PARENTING
Teens

7 Steps to Escape Communication Breakdown
and Cultivate a Calm, Loving, Productive
Relationship with Your Teenager

DR CHRISTINA MARS

© Copyright 2024 - All rights reserved.

The content contained within this book may not be reproduced, duplicated or transmitted without direct written permission from the author or the publisher.

Under no circumstances will any blame or legal responsibility be held against the publisher, or author, for any damages, reparation, or monetary loss due to the information contained within this book. Either directly or indirectly.

Legal Notice:

This book is copyright protected. This book is only for personal use. You cannot amend, distribute, sell, use, quote or paraphrase any part, or the content within this book, without the consent of the author or publisher.

Disclaimer Notice:

Please note the information contained within this document is for educational and entertainment purposes only. All effort has been executed to present accurate, up to date, and reliable, complete information. No warranties of any kind are declared or implied. Readers acknowledge that the author is not engaging in the rendering of legal, financial, medical or professional advice. The content within this book has been derived from various sources. Please consult a licensed professional before attempting any techniques outlined in this book.

By reading this document, the reader agrees that under no circumstances is the author responsible for any losses, direct or indirect, which are incurred as a result of the use of information contained within this document, including, but not limited to, — errors, omissions, or inaccuracies.

Contents

Introduction 1

Chapter 1. Strengthening Connections: Steps towards a Calmer, More Productive, and Loving Relationship 5
- Step 1: Practice Active Listening 6
- Step 2: Establish Trust 9
- Step 3: Encourage and Bolster Self-Esteem ... 11
- Step 4: Set Boundaries 14
- Step 5: Practice Emotional Intelligence and be a Positive Role Model 16
- Step 6: Encourage Open Dialogue 18
- Step 7: Maintain Connection 20

Chapter 2. Mission Possible - Decoding Your Teenager's World 23
- The Developing Teenage Brain: An Overview 27
- The Prefrontal Cortex: The Decision-Making Hub 29
- The Limbic System: The Emotional Roller Coaster 30

- The Teenage Brain and Impulsivity....... 32
- The Social Impact on the Teenage Brain... 34
- Understanding Change and Growth in the Teenage Brain 35

Chapter 3. Nurturing a Healthy Lifestyle for Your Teen................................. 37
- Developing Healthy Eating Patterns 39
- Developing Healthy Sleep Habits and Routines........................... 44
- Promoting Physical Health and Wellness.. 47
- The Impact of Social Media on Teenagers' Lives 49
- Encouraging Mindfulness and Stress Management Techniques 55

Chapter 4. Building Strong Bonds: Steps to a Stronger Family 61
- Balancing Work and Family Life: Finding Harmony in a Busy World 63
- Sibling Dynamics and Conflict Resolution... 67
- Supporting Your Teen Through Divorce and Family Changes................. 69

Chapter 5. Navigating Challenges in Your Teens' Mental Health....................... 75
- Adolescent Mental Health & Anxiety: Recognizing and Addressing Concerns.... 78

Chapter 6. Setting Boundaries and Dealing with Substance Use, Addiction, and Other Risk-Taking Behaviors.................. 92
- Drugs............................... 95
- Alcohol 103
- Tobacco/Nicotine Products 106
- Risk-Taking...................... 108
- Unprotected Sex.................... 111
- Dangerous Driving.................. 111
- Illegal Activities.................... 113
- Fighting........................... 115
- Truancy 117

Chapter 7. All About Friendships, Relationships, and Sex 122
- Friendships 123
- Teen Relationships, Sexuality, and Consent.. 127

Chapter 8. Supporting Your Teen's Education and Empowering Them for the Future....... 134
- Academic Pressure and College Choices: Encouraging a Balanced Perspective..... 136
- Fostering Responsibility and Independence: Preparing Teens for Adulthood 139
- Essential Life Skills-Financial Literacy and Money Management: Paving the Path to Financial Independence........ 143

- Encouraging Leadership and Community Involvement: Nurturing the Next Generation of Leaders and Active Citizens . . 145
- Resilience and Coping Skills: Equipping Your Teen for Life's Hurdles. 148

Chapter 9. Building a Lasting Connection: The Parent-Teenager Relationship in Adulthood **154**

- Moving from Parenting to Mentoring . . . 157
- Supporting Your Teen's Personal and Professional Goals 159
- Nurturing Emotional Intimacy and Open Communication 161
- Engaging in Shared Interests and Activities 163
- Respecting Boundaries and Privacy in Adult Relationships 165

Introduction

It's 3 am when most of the world is asleep. But for me, sleep seems like a distant memory. I'm sitting in my living room, cradling a cup of cold tea, my heart pounding so hard that I can hear its echo in the silence. We've just returned from the local police station, where we had to pick up our 13-year-old son Ted, who decided to take our car for an unsanctioned late-night adventure.

As I stared into the untouched cup of tea, the officer's words replay, "He's safe, but I think he was trying to impress some friends." I found myself grappling with a whirlwind of emotions - relief, frustration, confusion, and a profound sense of helplessness. I thought I knew my child, but this incident made me question everything.

My son, once a sweet, if a little boisterous, child, is now a teenager on the precipice of adulthood. I realize that the transformation is physical but also emotional and psychological. With each passing day, it seems like he is drifting further away, hiding behind a wall of silence and indifference. The tender conversations have been replaced with monosyllabic grunts, and the shared laughter seems like a memory from another lifetime.

This was six years ago. I understand the challenges you're going through. I, too, experience the slammed doors, the one-word answers, the endless negotiation about screen time, and the heart-wrenching feeling that your once affectionate child has become a stranger. Parenting a teenager can feel like navigating a minefield blindfolded. You step gingerly, praying you don't trip a wire, but you do all too often. And the following explosion leaves everyone hurt and even more distant than before.

You've likely read countless parenting books and spoken to friends, family, or professionals, yet the solution eludes you. The gap between you and your teenager seems ever widening, and you're desperate to bridge it.

You're tired, frustrated, and scared. Afraid that this disconnect might become permanent, your child might carry the pain of these tumultuous years into adulthood or, worse, pass it on to their children someday. Above all, you're scared of losing them – not just physically, but emotionally.

Perhaps the catalyst that led you to this book was a particularly heated argument, an alarming report card, or maybe just the numbing silence that fills the space where laughter and conversation once were. It sparked an urgency in you to seek change, seek answers beyond the usual advice, and find a way to reconnect with your child.

You are here because you realize that a one-size-fits-all solution can't address this crucial phase of your child's life. You recognize that your child is unique, their situation is unique, and you need not just a manual but a map that considers the terrain you and your child are navigating. You're not looking for quick fixes or easy answers but for a deeper understanding of your teenager's world and the tools to build a bridge to that world. That's the gap this book aims to fill. This book took years of real-life experience raising teens to write. And I'm still in the thick of it, with children of 19, 16, and 11.

Imagine a world where your relationship with your teenager is not defined by conflict and frustration but by respect, open dialogue, and mutual understanding. A world where their mood swings and rebellion are not obstacles but doors to deeper connection and growth. A world where you guide and listen to them with a compassionate heart that seeks to understand their struggles and support their dreams. I'm not saying this is an easy path; it takes dedication and patience, and we will all make mistakes along the way, but by the time you turn the last page of this book, you'll be a parent to your teenager and their confidant and mentor. You'll be equipped to handle their emotional outbursts, academic challenges, and digital distractions.

This is not just a vision but a real possibility—a better life that awaits you and your teenager at the end of this journey. A life where you look back and know, without a doubt, that you did your best, and it made all the difference.

As a British-trained family doctor, I have witnessed firsthand the numerous and multifaceted issues that teenagers grapple with. I've sat across from them, listened to their worries, fears, and dreams, and guided them through their darkest hours. But it was only when I became a mother to teenagers that I fully appreciated the depth and complexity of our journey as parents.

The dual perspectives of a medical professional and a mother have given me a unique vantage point to provide you with advice. This book is the culmination of years of clinical experience and personal trials geared toward helping you navigate the often-rough waters of parenthood. The journey will likely be filled with mistakes, tough times, worry, and heartache. But we grow and learn through our resilience, empathy, respect, and willingness to accept when we get things wrong and apologize.

Before the recent advancements in neuroscience and psychology, our understanding of teenagers was mired in stereotypes and misconceptions. We saw rebellion, where there was a search for identity, disrespect, a need for autonomy, and apathy, where there was a struggle for meaning.

This book is tailor-made for parents like you who are determined to forge a deep, supportive connection with their teenagers. With its blend of evidence-based strategies, real-life anecdotes, and empathetic understanding, you'll learn how to navigate the challenges of the teenage years and help your child flourish. This is the key to unlocking a fulfilling, even at times harmonious, relationship with your teen, ensuring you both grow and thrive during this transformative stage of life.

CHAPTER 1

Strengthening Connections: Steps towards a Calmer, More Productive, and Loving Relationship

Parenting teenagers can sometimes feel like navigating through a maze with no map - a perplexing and challenging phase that often leaves you unsure of the path forward. Sometimes, you think you can't fix this relationship and find it perplexing, frustrating, and sometimes even sad.

My son is now an adult and calls me regularly for chats and advice. We talk more than we ever did when he was a teenager. Nina is 16, and we are in the thick of it. I am sure many of you know what I am talking about. We have our good days and our bad days. My youngest, Tess, is 11, and I remain worried about her teenage years to come. I have distilled the lessons I've learned on this journey in this book. There are no easy answers, no quick fixes. This is a road map that I have to remind myself of constantly and that I continually refer to, and I am excited to share it with you.

In this chapter, I will introduce you to my 7-step method, a comprehensive approach designed to help you enhance communication and cultivate a more nurturing relationship with your teen. This method isn't a quick-fix solution or a one-size-fits-all answer but a roadmap to guide you and, even more importantly, a process adaptable to your family's unique dynamics.

Step 1: Practice Active Listening

Listening is honestly one of the greatest acts of love. Active listening is the bedrock upon which strong, trusting relationships are built. In the context of parenting, it's the key that opens the door to your teenager's world, enabling you to understand their experiences, concerns, and aspirations truly. It means going beyond merely hearing their words and genuinely listening to their feelings and unspoken messages.

As simple as it sounds, active listening requires practice. It's more than just being silent while your teen talks or giving them an open ear. It's about offering your undivided attention, demonstrating understanding, and validating their feelings. It's about being there, in the moment, fully invested in the conversation, and showing them through your actions that their voice matters.

Active listening begins with creating a safe and comfortable space for conversation. Choose a quiet, private location free from distractions where your teen feels at ease. Give your teen your full attention. Put away your devices, maintain eye contact, and listen carefully to what they're saying. This shows your teenager that you value their opinions and perspectives, reinforcing their self-worth and fostering their confidence to express themselves. I know we all lead busy lives, and time is a factor, but remember, this doesn't always need to be a long stint; as long as the listening is quality, any amount of time you give them is valuable.

When your teen shares something with you, avoid the temptation to jump in with your solutions or advice immediately. This is something I continue to struggle with and practice daily. I'm a fixer and like to come up with solutions and advice. Resist! Instead, show empathy by acknowledging their feelings. Respond with phrases like, "I can see why you're upset" or "That must have been difficult for you." This validates their feelings and signals that it's okay for them to express themselves, even if their experiences or emotions are challenging.

As you listen, be mindful of your reactions and body language. How you respond non-verbally can significantly impact how comfortable your teen feels in sharing their thoughts and feelings and how far they will be prepared to go. Maintain a calm demeanor, nod your head in understanding, and keep your body language open and receptive.

Asking open-ended questions is another vital aspect of active listening. These questions require more than a simple yes or no answer, prompting your teen to explore and articulate their thoughts more deeply. For instance, instead of asking, "Did you have a good day at school?" which can be answered with a mere 'yes' or 'no,' try asking, "What was the most interesting thing that happened at school today?" or even "Were you able to help somebody at school today?" These questions allow your teen to share their experiences, thoughts, and feelings fully.

However, while asking questions can be helpful, you must avoid interrogating your teen or making them feel like they're on trial. The aim is to foster an open dialogue, not to cross-examine them. Let the conversation flow naturally and follow their lead.

Also, remember that it's okay if there are moments of silence in your conversation. Silence can provide a breathing space, a moment for your teen to gather their thoughts and feelings before they continue.

Above all, be patient. Open and genuine communication may take time to happen. It's a process that takes time and patience. Active listening will pave the way for more meaningful and open conversations with your teen.

Recall your own experiences of being a teenager. Even relay them to your child. This will allow you to empathize with your teenager more effectively and remind you of the importance of having someone to turn to who really listens.

Step 2: Establish Trust

The second vital step towards strengthening the bond with your teenager revolves around trust. Establishing and maintaining trust between a parent and a teenager is delicate. It requires patience, care, and a good deal of understanding.

Trust is built over time and anchored in reliability, consistency, and honesty. It forms a protective shell around the relationship, fostering a sense of security in your teen. When teens feel secure, they are more likely to open up, share their feelings, thoughts, fears, and dreams, and engage in honest, meaningful conversations.

Reliability is the first pillar of trust. Being reliable means following through with what you say you'll do. Ensure you're there if you promise to pick up your teenager after a late-night party. If you've committed to helping them with their project, set aside the time to do so. If you promised to be at that performance, show up. By keeping your word, you're teaching your teenagers that they can rely on you. It assures them that you'll be there when they need you, and this reliability fosters trust.

Consistency is equally important. While your teenager is navigating physical, emotional, and social changes, their world can often feel like it's in a state of constant flux, but by being consistent - in your actions, your behavior, your expectations, and your responses - you become a stable, dependable figure in their often-chaotic world. Consistency provides a sense of predictability and safety, which is comforting and reassuring to teenagers.

Honesty may be the most challenging characteristic, particularly when the truth is difficult or uncomfortable. However, honesty fosters respect, integrity, and trust in any relationship between a parent and a teenager. By being honest - about your feelings, mistakes, expectations, and experiences - you model a crucial value for your teen. However, remember that honesty should not be confused with harsh truth-telling. It's always essential to express honesty empathetically and with respect for your teenager's feelings and experiences.

A key aspect of establishing trust with your teenager is respecting their privacy. This involves developing a sense of personal identity and private space. Respecting their privacy doesn't mean you're in the dark about their lives. Instead, it means acknowledging and respecting their need for personal space and autonomy. It means knocking before entering their room, not snooping through their personal belongings, not reading their texts and checking their phone, and not insisting they share every detail of their lives with you. Of course, there may be some flexibility here, especially if their safety is at stake. Still, as a general rule, they must know their texts/phones and diaries are private and won't be violated.

Building trust also entails showing trust in your teenager. Trust is a two-way street; showing your teenager you trust them can strengthen your relationship. Whether trusting them to complete their family responsibilities (our family prefers that phrase to 'chores'), being responsible when they're out with friends, or making wise decisions, demonstrating your trust in them can foster their confidence and self-esteem. It also encourages them to live up to your expectations.

Building trust is a continuous process. It's not something that can be achieved overnight, and there will be times when this trust is tested or even broken, which you will see in later stories of my teen son Ted. When this happens, it's crucial to address the issue openly and honestly, to learn from the experience, and to work together to rebuild trust.

Trust is the solid ground upon which the relationship with your teenager stands. Establishing and maintaining trust will pave the way for open communication, mutual respect, and a strong, loving relationship with your teenager.

Step 3: Encourage and Bolster Self-Esteem

The third step in building a stronger bond with your teenager centers around bolstering and encouraging their self-esteem. They will grapple with their evolving identities, peer pressure, academic expectations, and the perils and pleasures of social media. As a parent, your role is instrumental in providing them with the validation and encouragement they need to navigate these years confidently.

Self-esteem is the bedrock of a person's mental and emotional health. It's the reflection they see when they look in the mirror of self-perception, influenced by their experiences and the feedback they receive from others, particularly from parents. Teenagers with high self-esteem feel confident about their abilities, values, and worth. They are more resilient, optimistic, and more likely to face challenges head-on.

You can bolster your teenager's self-esteem in several ways. Firstly, by offering praise where it's due. When your teenager accomplishes something - whether it's a significant achievement like scoring well on a test or a minor victory like helping with household responsibilities - acknowledge their effort and praise them. Remember to focus your praise on their effort, determination, and resilience rather than purely on the outcome. This way, they understand that their worth is not only tied to success but to the journey and effort as well. You may think this isn't necessary as they get older, but they need it more than at any other time in their childhood while not asking or appearing to need it.

Therefore, ensuring your praise is sincere and specific is crucial. General, non-specific praise like "good job" may feel insincere or hollow. Instead, try something like, "I appreciate how you spent so much time studying for your test. Your dedication shows." Specific praise makes your teenager feel seen and acknowledged for their efforts and actions.

Encouragement plays a complementary role to praise. While praise focuses on the achievements, encouragement zeroes in on the effort and the perseverance, especially in the face of difficulties. When your teenager faces a challenge - be it a tricky math problem, a conflict with a friend, or a setback in their hobby - be their cheerleader. Please encourage them to keep trying, to learn from their mistakes, and to believe in their capabilities. This type of encouragement boosts their confidence and cultivates resilience.

Acknowledging and validating their feelings and emotions is another powerful tool in bolstering self-esteem. Whether they're feeling proud, frustrated, excited, or even depressed or anxious, acknowledge it. This conveys the message that their feelings are important and that it's okay to express them.

Given our digital age, teenagers are also dealing with the pressures and complexities of social media. The virtual world can often distort reality, making teenagers question their self-worth as they compare themselves to the filtered lives they see online. Talk to your teenager about the impacts of social media (and there will be much more on this in Chapter 3). Remind them that their worth is not determined by their online presence or the number of likes or followers they have. If they are on social media, encourage them to engage with it mindfully and focus on real-life connections and experiences.

Remember to lead by example in bolstering your teenager's self-esteem. Model positive self-talk and healthy self-esteem. Show them, through your actions and attitudes, that everyone has strengths and weaknesses and that it's okay to make mistakes and learn from them.

Bolstering self-esteem and providing encouragement can significantly impact your teenager's overall development. It can foster a sense of self-belief, resilience, and positivity, empowering them to face the complexities of the teenage years with confidence. By offering praise, encouragement, validation, and support, you strengthen your bond with your teenager and contribute to their journey of self-discovery and growth.

Step 4: Set Boundaries

Setting boundaries is critical in fostering a healthy and respectful relationship with your teenager. Clear boundaries lay the framework for mutual understanding and respect, helping keep the relationship balanced. They also give your teenager a sense of structure and predictability, which can create a feeling of security.

When discussing setting boundaries, it's not just about rules or limitations. It's about defining a safe and respectful space for interaction, communication, and behavior. Boundaries should encompass a wide range of aspects, including physical boundaries (like personal space and privacy), emotional boundaries (respect for feelings, thoughts, and experiences), and behavioral boundaries (rules for actions and behaviors).

While it might be tempting to dictate these boundaries, involving your teen in decision-making is essential. This collaborative approach fosters a sense of ownership and responsibility in your teenager. It also respects their growing autonomy and demonstrates that you value their input.

In setting boundaries, begin with a calm and open conversation. Clearly define what behavior is acceptable and your family's expectations. It will be a dynamic process as your teenager grows and their needs and wants to evolve. Ensure that these expectations are realistic and age appropriate. Involving your teen in this will help them feel more invested.

Discuss the consequences of crossing these boundaries. These should be logical and related to the boundary that's been betrayed and must be something you are prepared to carry out. They should aim to teach your teen responsibility and the impact of their actions rather than punish them. Consequences don't always have to be negative (things taken away, privileges revoked); they can be more positive, action-based consequences, such as writing apologies, extra family responsibilities, volunteering, or helping an elderly neighbor. Try to get creative with them; it will be more rewarding.

Be aware that there will be instances where flexibility and compromise are needed. Flexibility is about acknowledging that there might be exceptions to the rules in certain situations. It's about finding a middle ground where you uphold the boundaries while respecting your teen's individuality.

Remember, the goal isn't to control your teenager but to guide them toward becoming a responsible, respectful, and empathetic individual. If your teenager presents a strong case for why a specific boundary should be changed or an exception should be made, be willing to listen, discuss, and compromise if appropriate.

Setting boundaries can be challenging, fraught with emotions and potential conflicts. But when approached with respect, open communication, mutual agreement, and consistency, it can significantly enhance your relationship with your teenager.

It also gives your teenager a predictable structure within which they can operate, providing them a sense of security and stability. Teenagers are going to push these boundaries. It's all part of this phase of development, and from personal experience, it will sometimes be hard to uphold the consequences. The more a feisty teenager is given clear boundaries, the better they will respond and understand, in the end, what you are trying to do and why.

Step 5: Practice Emotional Intelligence and be a Positive Role Model

Emotional intelligence is the ability to understand, manage, and effectively express our own feelings, as well as engage and navigate successfully with the feelings of others. In the context of parenting, it becomes the backbone of understanding and nurturing your teen's emotional health.

Understanding our own emotions is the first facet of emotional intelligence. As parents, we carry a complex web of emotions, often a blend of care, concern, frustration, and countless other feelings, many brought with us from our upbringing. Recognizing these emotions and how they impact our reactions is crucial. For example, you might be more likely to snap at your teen for a minor issue if you're stressed from work. Knowing this can help you manage your reactions better and respond more empathetically. Acknowledging to your teen that you responded in such a way because you had had a bad day is extremely powerful. So many children will otherwise have that lingering doubt in the back of their minds that it was their fault, which will negatively affect their self-esteem.

Similarly, if your teen has had a bad day at school, they, in turn, might be more prone to an emotional outburst.

Recognizing and discussing this is a powerful tool as they progress toward adulthood. Emotional intelligence also means trying to understand your teen and showing empathy. Remember, adolescence is a time of intense emotional changes, often marked by mood swings and heightened sensitivity. Understanding this can help you respond with kindness and patience.

Being a positive role model for your child involves managing your and your teen's emotions. This involves responding thoughtfully rather than reacting impulsively. For example, if your teen breaks a rule, rather than reacting out of anger, take a moment to calm down, take at least three breaths in through your nose and out through your mouth, or count to 10. Try to communicate then your feelings and the reason for any consequences in a composed way. This approach prevents heated arguments and teaches teens how to handle their emotions in challenging situations.

As parents, we're our teen's first and most influential role models. They learn more from observing our behavior than from listening to our advice. Therefore, it's essential to model healthy emotional behavior. This includes managing our emotions effectively, treating others with kindness and respect, being patient, and resolving conflicts maturely.

Demonstrating healthy coping strategies is also essential (more in Chapter 3). Show them how you manage stress - perhaps you meditate, practice yoga, walk, read a book, or talk about your feelings with a close friend. Encourage your teen to explore their healthy coping strategies. Support them in their endeavors, be it sports, arts, reading, or any other hobby that helps them relax and express themselves.

Finally, guide your teen when necessary. There will be instances when your teen might struggle to manage their emotions. In such cases, try to lend them a listening ear, empathize with their feelings, and guide them on how to cope with their emotions. Certainly, don't invalidate their feelings or offer unsolicited advice. Instead, let them know that it's okay to have intense emotions, and it's more about how we manage these emotions that matters.

Being emotionally intelligent and a positive role model is a continual learning process; we will only sometimes get it right. Instead, stay committed to understanding and managing emotions effectively and modeling the same for your teen.

Step 6: Encourage Open Dialogue

As we move through adolescence, conversations tend to move from simple requests or directives to complex discussions about life, morality, ambitions, fears, and dreams. This step aims to create a safe and inviting environment for your teen, where they feel valued and understood, fostering mutual respect.

Try to approach each conversation with an open mind and heart. Remember that each conversation is an opportunity to better understand your teen's world. It's not always about agreeing or disagreeing with their opinions but more about respecting their individuality and their right to express their thoughts. There is room for debate and teaching them a respectful way to listen is also extremely important. They may be developing different views to your own as they read, learn, and mature, which is an excellent exercise for a parent in listening to another point of view and responding thoughtfully.

Make sure to avoid imposing your views or criticizing their opinions. Instead, you can present your viewpoint as a suggestion or an alternative perspective for them to consider. This encourages your teen to think critically and make informed decisions while also showing them that you respect their autonomy as you move through the teen years into adulthood.

Involving your teen in family decisions can also promote open dialogue. Ask for their input and consider their opinions when making decisions that affect them. This shows that you value their viewpoint and encourage them to express their thoughts freely.

Ensure your teen knows they can talk to you about anything without fear of judgment or criticism. Keep the lines of communication open, even if they sometimes seem uninterested or distant. Just knowing that you're there for them can make a big difference.

And don't forget that even in those situations where your teenager asks you a crucial question or asks for advice just as you are rushing off to a meeting, even if you give them a few minutes and then be very open about how you have to go but would like to revisit this later or tomorrow (try and give a specific time and stick to it) that will be okay. Don't go off to your meeting drowning in guilt. Even though it seems they believe the world revolves around them and them alone, they are old enough to understand that schedules are schedules, and sometimes the more extended discussion may need to be postponed.

Step 7: Maintain Connection

The last step is perhaps one of the most fundamental components of a healthy parent-teen relationship – maintaining a meaningful connection. Even with greater independence, realizing that this doesn't mean they don't need you anymore is crucial. They still crave connection, just in different ways.

Quality time is at the heart of maintaining a connection with your teenager. While it can be challenging, particularly with busy schedules and social commitments, prioritizing this time together is paramount. But how can you do this effectively?

Begin by actively participating in activities that your teenager enjoys. If your teen loves music, listen to their favorite songs with them, discuss the lyrics, listen to them playing their instrument (even when you have ten million other things on your 'to do' list), or even attend a concert together. If they are into sports, offer to help them practice at home and cheer them on at their matches. Sharing these experiences creates common ground, a shared language that brings you closer and deepens your understanding of one another.

I cannot put this strongly enough: attend their significant events. Whether it's a school play, a soccer match, or a debate competition, showing up for them signifies your support and validation, affirming that they matter to you. It will have a profound impact that they will never forget; you showed up, and the power of that I can't express enough.

Regular family dinners are another excellent and vital opportunity for connection. Despite the digital era where devices can creep into mealtime, insist on device-free meals. These gatherings allow everyone to come together and share their day, the highs and lows, and anything in between. It fosters an environment of open communication and will enable you to stay in tune with your teen's life.

Chapter Takeaways:

1. Practice Active Listening: The cornerstone of effective communication with your teenager. Active listening involves more than just hearing; it involves fully understanding and validating your teen's emotions and thoughts.

2. Establish Trust: Built on the pillars of reliability, consistency, and honesty, trust forms the backbone of a solid parent-teen relationship.

3. Bolster Self-Esteem and Encouragement: Boosting your teen's self-esteem through sincere

praise and encouragement can significantly improve their well-being.

4. Set Boundaries: Collaboratively setting clear, realistic, and flexible boundaries fosters mutual respect and provides a secure environment for your teenager.

5. Practice Emotional Intelligence and Be a Positive Role Model: Being emotionally aware and a good role model can help you and your teen manage emotions effectively, ultimately strengthening your relationship.

6. Encourage Open Dialogue: Creating a safe and open environment for conversation allows for meaningful discussions that respect your teen's growing autonomy and individuality.

7. Maintain Connection: Quality time and active involvement in your teen's interests are crucial for maintaining a strong emotional bond.

CHAPTER 2

Mission Possible - Decoding Your Teenager's World

A few years ago, ongoing worry about my son and his sometimes-dubious choices took on new meaning when he suddenly decided to organize a fight club at his high school. Using an out-of-bounds location, he had discovered while temporarily on crutches with the privilege of an elevator key, my son decided to create an arena for unregulated fights. What could have spurred him to pursue such a reckless endeavor? And this wasn't an isolated incident – countless times, he indulged in behavior that appeared utterly inexplicable from an adult perspective.

The teenage years really can be like a wild roller coaster ride. It was a stark reminder that we, as parents, despite our experience and wisdom, can be surprised by our children's actions, especially during their teenage years.

This led me to the question that would become the foundation of this chapter: How can we decode the labyrinth that is the teenage mind? It seemed essential to me to give you some explanation as to why teenagers can behave the way that they do. This chapter aims to offer some insight into the complexities of teenage brain development, the fascinating science behind their sometimes-baffling behaviors, and the physiological changes they undergo. Even though this does not offer practical advice like the rest of the book, it will give you more understanding and may give you pause for thought when reacting, and even a beat can make a world of difference.

The focus will be on demystifying why teens make seemingly irrational decisions, why their moods swing like a pendulum, and why risk and thrill-seeking behaviors become their new norm. We will explore the development of the prefrontal cortex and its role in decision-making, as well as the function of the limbic system and its impact on emotional response.

We can gain valuable insights into our teenagers' world by investigating adolescence's scientific and psychological aspects. This understanding will be a powerful tool, enabling us to guide them better, offer appropriate support, and respond effectively during this crucial life phase.

I understand this may be more information than you have the time or inclination to read. Therefore, I have flipped this chapter and started with the chapter takeaways. This way, you grasp the basics before heading on to Chapter 3 and can always go back and dive into more detail later if time allows.

Chapter Takeaways:

1. The Teenage Brain is a Work in Progress: The brain continues to develop into a person's late 20s through a process of myelination (insulation) of neurons, and the teenage years are a crucial phase for this, a process that starts at the back of the brain and moves forward to the prefrontal cortex. Understanding the ongoing development of the prefrontal cortex helps explain why teenagers can be impulsive, make seemingly irrational moves, and make decisions based more strongly on their emotions.

2. Limbic System and Emotions: The limbic system, responsible for emotional processing, is more active in teenagers. This explains their heightened emotional sensitivity and mood swings, which are expected at this stage in their development.

3. Synaptic Plasticity and Learning: The teenage brain is highly adaptable, undergoing a process of 'pruning' to become more efficient. This makes teenagers incredibly receptive to new experiences and learning but also susceptible to environmental influences, both good and bad.

4. Impact of Social Experiences: The teenage brain is susceptible to social cues, and peer influence plays a significant role in their brain development. This has both positive and negative implications, especially in the context of social media.

5. Stress and Impulsivity: The teenage brain has heightened responses to stress, which can exacerbate their impulsive behaviors. Understanding this can help parents guide teenagers through emotionally charged situations.

6. The Importance of Empathy and Guidance: Understanding the neurological basis of teenage behavior allows for more empathetic parenting. It provides a scientific basis for patience and helps us as parents' guide our children effectively through this challenging phase.

7. Unveiling the Enigma: This chapter underscores that understanding the teenage brain is not impossible. With this knowledge, parents can replace exasperation with empathy, ultimately fostering an environment where teenagers can grow and thrive.

The Developing Teenage Brain: An Overview

The concept of a brain growing, and maturing might be something you have not often thought about, but it's a vital part of human development. Unlike other organs in our bodies that are generally fully developed by our early teenage years, the brain takes longer to reach its full potential. That journey can stretch into a person's late 20s, and it's the last organ of the body to develop fully. This is the fascinating realm of neurodevelopment, and the teenage brain is at the epicenter of these transformations.

Let's envision the brain's development like a sprawling, bustling city, constantly under construction, to make sense of this. The foundations are laid down in childhood, while adolescence is a period of rapid construction, creating a network of roads, buildings, and infrastructures.

The back regions of our brain, responsible for essential functions like motor control and visual processing, mature first. Gradually, the maturation process progresses towards the front of the brain, the frontal lobe, where the prefrontal cortex resides at the very front. This region, often called the command center, is responsible for complex cognitive processes, such as planning, decision-making, and social behavior.

What causes the maturation of the brain? The answer lies in a process called myelination. Imagine for a moment that the neurons in our brains are like a city's electrical wires. Myelin, a fatty white substance, acts like the insulation around the wires, ensuring the rapid and efficient transfer of electrical signals between neurons. It's this myelination process that underpins the maturation and development of our brains.

Myelination starts at birth and continues into adulthood but follows a specific pattern. It begins in the back of the brain and gradually progresses to the front. This means the last part of the brain to myelinate fully is the prefrontal cortex, which is crucial for high-level thinking and decision-making.

During the teenage years, the prefrontal cortex is still developing and myelinating. As a result, it's not yet operating at full capacity. The partial myelination leads to an imbalance between the emotional brain, which develops earlier, and the rational brain, which lags behind. This imbalance can often explain why teenagers are prone to making impulsive decisions or struggle with understanding the long-term consequences of their actions. Sound familiar?

When the myelination of the prefrontal cortex isn't fully complete, it's like trying to use a high-speed broadband service with an outdated dial-up modem. The information might still get there, but it's not as quick or efficient. This lag can explain why teenagers often act on impulse or struggle with risk assessment. This information was like a light bulb going off for me, living with my risk-searching son. Although it was still hard to live with the constant worry of whatever would happen next, it reassured me this wouldn't necessarily last a lifetime. As parents, we can draw on this understanding to better appreciate our teenager's world. It's like decoding a complex but rewarding puzzle. The seemingly erratic actions and mood swings become a little more comprehensible when we view them through the lens of brain development. And with this newfound understanding, we can create an environment that is supportive, nurturing, and conducive to their successful navigation of these transformational years.

The Prefrontal Cortex: The Decision-Making Hub

When it comes to the brain, the prefrontal cortex plays a role much like the CEO of your brain. Its position at the front of the brain directs the thoughts, actions, and emotions we experience daily. It's an integral part of what makes us human, overseeing executive functions such as decision-making, empathy, risk assessment, and impulse control.

The term 'executive functions' might sound official and intimidating, but it refers to high-level mental skills that help us get things done, including the all-important homework and papers that need organization, time management, and focus on completing.

With an underdeveloped prefrontal cortex, which, as we now know, is the last part of the brain to reach full maturity, teenagers may struggle with impulse control and decision-making, much like a young company with a novice CEO. This mismatch between a still-developing brain and a world full of choices and greater independence can lead to what we often recognize as typical teenage behavior: impulsive decisions, risk-taking, and a perceived lack of judgment.

In addition to maturation, the teenage brain is also undergoing a fascinating process known as synaptic plasticity. In childhood, the brain creates many of these pathways (like the electrical wires I mentioned earlier), but not all of them will be maintained. This is where synaptic plasticity and the concept of 'pruning' come into play.

During adolescence, the brain begins to prune away the lesser-used pathways, much like a gardener would prune away the less healthy branches of a tree to strengthen the rest. The pathways that see more traffic become more robust, efficient, and better insulated, much like a well-trodden path in a forest.

This process of strengthening and pruning leads to a more streamlined and effective neural network. But what does this mean for our teenagers? It means their brains are incredibly receptive to new experiences and learning. They are hardwired to soak up information, adapt, and grow. This is why teenagers can pick up new skills or languages faster than adults and why their experiences during these years profoundly impact their development.

The Limbic System: The Emotional Roller Coaster

Have you ever wondered why teenagers often seem to be riding an emotional roller coaster, their moods swinging wildly from euphoria to despair in a matter of moments? The answer lies deep within their brains, in an area known as the limbic system.

The limbic system is a complex network of structures tucked underneath the cerebral cortex (the main body of the brain) and above the brainstem, functioning as the brain's emotional processing center. Two components of this area are the amygdala and the hippocampus. The amygdala is responsible for the control of emotions and behavior and also regulates anxiety and aggression. The hippocampus, a seahorse-shaped structure, is essential for memory formation and processing of emotions.

In adolescence, the limbic system takes center stage. Because the prefrontal cortex is still maturing, teenagers rely more heavily on the limbic system for decision-making. But there's a catch. The structures within the limbic system, especially the amygdala, are closely tied to emotions and the brain's reward and pleasure centers. As a result, teens often base their decisions on emotional responses rather than rational thought. This brain-based quirk can lead to actions driven by immediate gratification, leading to decisions that bewilder adults. My son's late-night car ride springs to the forefront of my mind!

However, this increased activity in the limbic system is not without purpose. The teenage years are a time of heightened emotional sensitivity, much of it necessary for social bonding and self-discovery. During this time, teens develop a more profound capacity for empathy, allowing them to understand and share the feelings of others more effectively. This process, while challenging, is vital to their journey into adulthood and the formation of their identities.

This heightened emotional sensitivity can also lead to what many parents recognize as characteristic teenage behavior: dramatic emotional outbursts and mood swings. One minute, your teen might laugh and joke; the next, they may retreat into sullen silence or explode in anger. These emotional swings can be perplexing and, at times, exhausting for both the teen and the people around them, but they are part of the normal process of adolescence.

Understanding the limbic system's role in your teenager's emotional responses can provide valuable insights into their behavior. This awareness can foster empathy and patience, which are crucial for maintaining open lines of communication. By recognizing the origins of their emotional intensity, you can better support them with greater understanding.

The Teenage Brain and Impulsivity

When observing teenagers, their occasional inability to resist sudden whims and risky decisions may seem baffling to adults. The unique interplay of the developing areas of their brains leads to this characteristic impulsivity.

Teenagers' propensity for impulsive behavior is primarily driven by this uneven pace of brain development that we've already talked about. This imbalance, if you like, is most apparent when teenagers face thrilling or risky decisions. Under such circumstances, the promise of immediate pleasure or social acceptance, both processed in the limbic system, will override the prefrontal cortex's weak voice of caution, or at least the connection is too slow for that area to have a significant influence on that decision. Consequently, teenagers may disregard potential negative consequences, choosing actions that yield immediate rewards.

Understanding the teen brain requires a closer look at the reward circuits in their brains. Our brains have evolved to seek and respond to rewards. Dopamine, a neurotransmitter often called the 'feel-good' chemical, plays a significant role in the brain's reward system. In response to perceived rewards, the brain releases dopamine, creating feelings of pleasure and satisfaction.

In the teenage brain, this reward system is in overdrive. Their brain is wired to seek new experiences and rewards, making them naturally more inclined to take risks. When teenagers perceive a reward— social acceptance, an adrenaline rush, or a unique experience—their brain responds by releasing dopamine. This potent rush of dopamine often drowns out the cautionary notes from the still-maturing prefrontal cortex, leading to impulsive decisions and risk-taking behavior.

This relationship between the developing prefrontal cortex and the hypersensitive reward system sheds light on why teenagers seem particularly prone to risky behavior. However, understanding this dynamic doesn't imply that such behavior should be condoned or dismissed as 'just a phase.' Instead, it allows us to guide teenagers toward healthier decision-making.

Stress also uniquely affects the teenage brain and can exacerbate impulsivity. Adolescents tend to have heightened responses to stress, with their brains triggering intense emotional reactions. When stressed, a teenager's brain might bypass the rational prefrontal cortex and rely on the more reactionary limbic system for decision-making.

This response mechanism can lead to impulsive decisions, as stress disrupts the brain's normal decision-making processes. Consequently, teenagers may make rash decisions in an attempt to alleviate the immediate stress, again highlighting the weight placed on immediate rewards.

The Social Impact on the Teenage Brain

During the teenage years, social experiences significantly influence brain development. As we have learned, the adolescent brain is constantly in flux, a work-in-progress where structures and connections are being built, reshaped, and strengthened. The brain is highly adaptable in this phase and sensitive to experiences, especially social ones.

Take, for instance, the phenomenon of peer influence. The heightened importance teenagers place on their peers is not merely a social trend. It's a manifestation of underlying neurological processes. The teenage brain is primed for learning and adapting to its environment, including the social environment. Experiences with peers and the desire for social acceptance can directly impact the development of various brain regions, including those responsible for understanding others' perspectives and emotions.

As teenagers navigate their social world, they're learning to process complex social cues, understand emotional nuances, and empathize with others. These experiences can strengthen neuronal connections related to social cognition and emotional understanding. On the flip side, negative social experiences such as bullying or social isolation can lead to heightened stress responses and can have detrimental effects on the developing brain.

In understanding the social impact on the teenage brain, we gain a more nuanced picture of adolescence in the modern age. We see how the brain's development is not an isolated process but deeply intertwined with the social experiences that fill a teenager's world.

Understanding Change and Growth in the Teenage Brain

The impressive learning capacity of the teenage brain, combined with the heightened emotions and social sensitivities of this age, means teenagers are uniquely poised to grow from their experiences. Their brains are primed to learn from triumphs, failures, joy and sadness, love and loss. In doing so, they are building the groundwork for emotional intelligence, resilience, empathy, and many other skills that will serve them well in adulthood.

Yet, it's important to remember that with great potential comes great vulnerability. The teenage brain's remarkable adaptability makes it more susceptible to environmental influences, both good and bad. Teenagers, therefore, need guidance and support from the adults in their lives to navigate this period of change and growth.

Understanding and embracing these changes can make all the difference in a teenager's journey. It can transform how we approach teenage behaviors, replacing fear and misunderstanding with compassion and respect. We can be more understanding and supportive when we view their behaviors not as signs of rebellion or laziness but as manifestations of their unique brain development. I know it's not easy to do, as with all of this comes some intense frustration as a parent. Hang in there, keep consulting the seven steps; and one thing I also found invaluable was to talk with other mothers of teenagers for mutual support and relief. Ultimately, understanding change and growth in the teenage brain is about more than just comprehending biological processes. It's about acknowledging the marvels and complexities of this period of life, extending empathy toward teenagers, and recognizing their potential.

CHAPTER 3

Nurturing a Healthy Lifestyle for Your Teen

It felt essential to me to have this chapter front and center. The more we can nurture and instill the idea of a healthy lifestyle for our teens, the better and the more likely they are to take what they have learned into adulthood.

In this chapter, I emphasize the value of active listening and establishing trust as we guide our teens toward a balanced diet, regular physical activity, good sleep hygiene, and stress management techniques. By doing so, we nurture not just their physical well-being but also their emotional and cognitive health.

As parents, we must try to demonstrate the habits we want to see in our teens as much as possible within the constraints of our busy, hectic lives. Whether eating a balanced diet or incorporating physical exercise into our routine, our actions speak louder than words. Nurturing a healthy lifestyle for our teens by actively supporting them in building positive habits will enhance their physical, emotional, and cognitive well-being and set the foundation for a lifelong healthy lifestyle.

There's a well-known saying that 'health is wealth.' Good health doesn't merely mean the absence of disease; it implies the overall well-being of an individual, encompassing physical, mental, and social dimensions. The teen years are crucial for our children to embrace a healthy lifestyle as the habits developed during this period significantly influence their future health and lifestyle choices.

Whether setting the dinner table with colorful vegetables, going for a family hike, ensuring they get ample sleep, or teaching them how to breathe deeply when stressed, our involvement as parents is integral. Modeling these behaviors is the most valuable thing we can do as they might follow suit, but not necessarily immediately. I know this seems like an unattainable goal, especially with the pressures on teenagers and our busy lives, but even if you can take one thing from this chapter and incorporate or add it into your daily life, it will have made this chapter worthwhile, and a resource you can keep returning to.

I can't overplay the significance of a calm mind in maintaining good health. I'm not saying that I ever or very rarely achieve this. But I think about it often and do yoga once a week. At least it's a reset for me that has proved incredibly valuable. Trying to foster an environment that promotes mental peace and reduces stress levels is so important. Again, how does that work when you've done your 3rd ride since after school and still need to get dinner on the table? I get it. But even if this gets you thinking about how you might shift things even a little to create more calm, I will have done my job here.

In the following sections, we'll look into these facets in detail. We'll learn about fostering healthy eating habits and sleep patterns, promoting physical wellness, the impact of social media, and the role of mindfulness in managing stress.

Developing Healthy Eating Patterns

Eating well is about more than just the food on our plates. It's about the patterns we establish, our choices, and our attitudes toward nutrition. Developing healthy eating patterns is pivotal for teens as it shapes their food choices and dietary habits in adulthood.

Healthy eating is not about dietary limitations or depriving yourself of foods you love. It's about consuming a balanced diet rich in the nutrients your body needs to function optimally. This includes a variety of fruits, vegetables, lean proteins, and whole grains (rather than refined grains). It also means minimizing the intake of processed foods, unhealthy fats, and added sugars and watching drinks, many of which are high in sugar.

Healthy eating also incorporates the concept of intuitive eating, which means listening to your body's cues. Eat (slowly) when you're hungry and stop when you're full. It's about recognizing your body's signals and responding appropriately rather than following a rigid plan. This approach can be especially beneficial for teenagers who are still growing and have fluctuating energy needs.

For teenagers, caloric intake varies based on age, sex, physical activity, and individual metabolic rate. Generally, teenage boys require between 2,500 and 3,000 calories daily, while teenage girls need around 2,200 to 2,400 calories daily. It's important to meet these caloric needs, as much as possible, through nutrient-dense foods rather than empty calories like sugary snacks or fast food.

A balanced day might consist of three main meals—breakfast, lunch, and dinner—supplemented by two snacks.

When choosing snacks, encourage your teen to select snacks rich in nutrients. Here are some healthy snack ideas:

- Apple slices with nut butter
- Greek yogurt with fresh berries
- Carrot and cucumber sticks with hummus
- A handful of mixed nuts
- Rice cakes with avocado
- Smoothies made from fruits and vegetables

However, fostering these habits in our teens is easier said than done. Teenagers are notorious for their inclination towards junk food, dislike for anything 'green,' and unpredictable eating schedules. These unhealthy patterns pose significant health risks, including obesity, poor brain development, lethargy, and increased susceptibility to illnesses. For the longest time, I tried to get my son interested in food, even food preparation, thinking that handling the ingredients may cause him to be more invested. But no! Even to this day, he resists cooking despite a considerable amount of perseverance on my part. What he has developed, and I like to think that what I cooked and the produce I brought into our house had something to do with it, is very healthy eating habits. Long gone are the cookies and Doritos and junk food he sought out at a certain point. He gradually realized they were empty calories that didn't fill him up and, more importantly, did not support his sporting ambitions.

If you can prepare meals with your teen, allowing them to suggest foods and experiment with different recipes, this can ignite their interest in nutrition. Placing nutritious snack options within easy reach and keeping unhealthy foods out of the house can direct them toward healthier choices. I certainly have had much more success involving my daughters in cooking, creating, and baking in the kitchen. Don't worry if they are not interested- modeling cooking and eating with fresh, healthy ingredients will have an impact in the long term.

You can openly discuss the importance of nutrition and offer meal choices rather than imposing a set menu, and get your teens involved in meal choices for the week. Even suggest, as they age, preparing and cooking one meal for the family per week/month. This will increase their confidence in the kitchen and give them a sense of responsibility and achievement. They will also build up a repertoire of recipes they can make, equipping them to sustain themselves beyond the family home. Make sure to compliment them when that meal gets to the table-you didn't have to cook. That's huge!

Make it a general rule to have nutritious meals at home and limit the availability of processed snacks and ordering in. However, it also allows occasional indulgences to maintain a balanced perspective on food. Do not comment on calories in certain foods, especially if they embark on a treat. And absolutely do not comment on their body shape, around a discussion of food or not; teenagers are incredibly sensitive about this, and this could cause a massive dent in their self-esteem.

If your teen expresses concerns or new interests in specific diets or foods, listen and offer to explore those options together, provided they are healthy choices. Certain specialty diets can lead teens down an unhealthy road with eating habits. Be aware that the impact of social media on unhealthy eating patterns and diets can be particularly prevalent among girls. Being aware of this influence can help to encourage your teen to continue healthy eating patterns.

Education plays a significant role in shaping eating habits, especially in teenagers. One way to encourage your teens to develop healthy habits is to give them access to valuable resources. Consider providing them with educational books or magazines on nutrition but be aware that much of the information your teens will glean about nutrition and food, particularly for girls, will be from social media. The sites and posts they find are not necessarily reviewed or reliable sources. It will need careful and diplomatic communication to unpack certain facts that may need to be corrected. One positive thing about some social media apps is that recipes and hacks for delicious meals and snacks can be found and may encourage your teen into the kitchen; it certainly has with my daughter Nina.

Online articles from reputable sources such as the Mayo Clinic or the American Heart Association can provide quick insights into healthy living. Understanding the nutritional value of foods and how the body uses this energy can empower them to make informed decisions. They may have learned some of this at school, but nutrition education could be better in many districts.

For those who enjoy hands-on learning, cookery books designed for teens can be a great asset. Titles like "Teens Cook: How to Cook What You Want to Eat" by Megan and Jill Carle or "The Complete Cookbook for Young Chefs" by America's Test Kitchen can make the experience educational and fun. Learning to prepare their meals not only teaches them about nutrition but also equips them with a valuable life skill. Again, the recipes they want to try will likely come from TikTok and Instagram. Embrace them coming to the table with fresh ideas and encourage them to try new recipes.

Watch your teenagers' eating habits. Make sure they're eating breakfast and check in about school lunch. The key is to eat balanced meals regularly, eat intuitively, and complement dietary habits with regular physical activity. One parenting tool I brought with me from childhood was to finish everything on your plate. I wish I had never embarked on that idea with my children. Having your children listen to their bodies as they eat a meal relatively slowly and stop when they feel full is far better. Speed is important. Eat too fast, and their body's cues won't have time to kick in, and before you know it, they have eaten more than they need and could become bloated or uncomfortable, likely impacting their next meal. I am still slightly obsessed with not wasting food now; instead of having my children finish that food, I package it away and eat the leftovers for my lunch the next day!

Remember, healthy habits don›t develop overnight. The key is ensuring that «treat or party food» choices (for instance, pizzas, burgers, and fried chicken tenders) are seen as more treat foods than regular fixtures in their diet. As a parent, your role is to gently guide, educate, and create an environment conducive to healthy, intuitive eating.

Developing Healthy Sleep Habits and Routines

Adequate sleep is as fundamental to a teenager's wellbeing as a balanced diet and regular exercise. Unfortunately, it often falls by the wayside in the face of academic pressures, social commitments, technological distractions, and, of course, school schedules, which are not generally in line with the needs of teenagers. As parents, guiding our teens as much as possible toward a healthy sleep routine is crucial. But first, let's understand why teenagers need sleep and how much.

Sleep is essential for the healthy growth and development of teenagers. As we have already discussed, their bodies and brains are undergoing significant transformations, and they need ample rest to support these changes. On average, teens need about 8-10 hours of sleep each night. However, various factors can disrupt this sleep, leading to deprivation and ensuing consequences.

The causes of teenage sleep deprivation are many. Biological changes in the adolescent years cause a shift in the body's internal clock, pushing their natural sleep-wake cycle later. Early school start times, homework loads, extracurricular activities, part-time jobs, and social obligations can all reduce their sleep time. Further, the pervasive use of electronic devices late into the night disrupts their ability to fall asleep.

This deprivation affects teenagers on cognitive, emotional, physical, and behavioral levels. Lack of sleep can impair thinking, learning, and academic achievement. It also impacts emotional health, increasing the likelihood of mood swings, anxiety, and depression. Physically, sleep deprivation can slow growth, impair immunity, and increase the risk of accidents and injuries. It can also encourage risky behavior by impeding decision-making abilities.

To spot potential sleep problems, parents should look for signs like difficulty waking up in the morning, excessive daytime sleepiness, mood changes, academic issues, and increased caffeine use. Some teens might also suffer from sleep disorders, such as insomnia or sleep apnea, that require professional intervention.

Despite these challenges, there are strategies parents can employ to help their teens improve their sleep. Firstly, ensure they have a quiet, dark, and comfortable sleeping environment if possible. Reinforce the importance of a regular sleep schedule and encourage them to prioritize sleep. One effective strategy is to keep mobile phones out of the bedroom at night to minimize distractions and reduce exposure to blue light, which can interfere with sleep quality. Additionally, discourage using other electronic devices at least an hour before bedtime. If your teen struggles with sleep chronically, consider contacting a health professional for advice and support.

Fostering good sleep hygiene in our teens is a process, and setbacks are part of the journey. Encourage them to find a sleep routine that works for them and stick to it. As they grow and their commitments change, their sleep routines might need adjusting. Still, the fundamental principles remain the same - prioritize sleep, maintain a consistent schedule, and create a conducive sleep environment.

Discuss the importance of sleep openly and without judgment, inviting them to share their challenges in maintaining a sleep schedule. Trust their ability to understand their sleep needs while providing guidance.

If your teen is having difficulty sleeping, rather than prescribing a solution, ask them why they think they are not sleeping and what they believe could help. Sometimes, they may have insights into their sleep patterns that you haven't considered. Listen and don't rush to find a solution; help them find one themselves.

Promoting Physical Health and Wellness

Physical health and wellness go hand in hand with mental wellbeing, which is particularly crucial in the teenage years as our teens continue to build resilience.

Regular exercise helps build muscles, improves cardiovascular health, enhances mood, boosts cognitive function, and fosters a positive body image. It also lays the groundwork for healthy adult life and encourages a lifelong commitment to fitness.

The American Heart Association recommends that teens engage in at least 60 minutes of moderate to vigorous physical activity daily. A blend of different types of exercises is beneficial for overall health. This includes aerobic activities like running or biking for cardiovascular fitness, strength-training exercises for muscular development, flexibility exercises like yoga for range of motion, and mental benefits. Additionally, spending time in nature through activities like hiking, kayaking, or simply taking a walk in the neighborhood or local park can offer both physical and mental health benefits.

Encouraging physical activity in teenagers who aren't in organized sports can require creativity and persistence! While traditional sports like basketball or soccer are great, they aren't for everyone. Finding activities that your teen enjoys is critical to fostering long-term commitment. This could be dance classes, skateboarding, hiking, or online fitness programs. Turning physical activity into a fun and social experience can significantly boost participation and enjoyment. Model this yourself, even if you can only manage a walk in the neighborhood with your schedule. Even encourage your teen to come with you. It's a time to talk without direct eye contact and issues, thoughts, and worries that might not have been done otherwise can emerge. You could also go on a family hike once in a while or a bike ride if you have more time. Expect resistance when you first suggest this idea! But if you persevere, your teen may well be pleasantly surprised by the feeling it brings.

You can then make fitness what you might call a family value by modeling an active lifestyle and participating in activities together. Offering encouragement and positive feedback, setting manageable goals, and celebrating progress can also enhance their motivation.

There are many ways to boost physical activity in your teenager's daily routine. Encourage active transportation to and from school, like walking or biking, where possible. Support their participation in physical education classes at school or community sports programs. Ensure they take breaks from sedentary activities like studying or gaming to move around.

Remember, every bit of movement counts, and it's never too late to start. Even if your teen has been largely inactive, introducing physical activity can gradually bring positive changes. Start small, focus on enjoyment, and progressively increase the duration and intensity of the activity.

Promoting physical health and wellness in our teenagers is critical to their current and future health. By fostering a love for movement and respect for their bodies, we equip them with the tools to lead fulfilling, healthy, and active lives. Our role as parents is to guide, inspire, and support them in this journey, ensuring they understand that physical health is about feeling good and living well.

The Impact of Social Media on Teenagers' Lives

If you're a parent of a teenager today, it's impossible to ignore the role social media plays in their lives. As a parent, engaging with this and its influence is crucial. It is actively designed to be harmful in terms of its addictive component. Digital interactions and virtual connections have reshaped how adolescents perceive the world and themselves.

As a Mum, I've had my fair share of staying up late, scrolling through my teenager's Instagram/spam feeds, worrying about their exposure to harmful content, and wondering about their online interactions. If you've been through this, you're not alone. This violates the development of trust between you and your teen, and I soon gave this up and started approaching the issue in other ways.

Social media is a double-edged sword. On one hand, it allows teenagers to interact with their peers, express their thoughts, stay informed, and even learn. On the other hand, it poses potential risks that we, as parents, cannot afford to ignore.

Recent studies and reports, including a significant warning from the Surgeon General, highlight an alarming correlation between social media use and deteriorating mental health in teenagers. The advisory couldn't have been clearer: Our teens are suffering. Anxiety, depression, self-harm, and even suicidal ideation have been associated with excessive social media use.

Our teens are submerged in a sea of likes, comments, shares, and follows, which, while seemingly innocent, can harbor deep-seated psychological consequences. As the duration of screen time increases, so does the risk of mental health disorders. This revelation is chilling.

But the impacts don't end with deteriorating mental health. Social media presents an idealized, carefully curated version of reality, an illusion of perfection that can profoundly affect a teen's self-image and potentially precarious self-esteem. Imagine, as a teenager, scrolling through an endless feed of perfect bodies, glamorous lifestyles, and phenomenal successes. This unattainable reality can be detrimental, leading to negative self-perception, body image issues, and even triggering eating disorders. It's a damaging cycle that our children are unsuspectingly being drawn into.

A further grim aspect of the virtual world is cyberbullying. This form of bullying is pervasive and unrelenting, and its effects are devastating. As a mother and a doctor, I've seen how harmful words thrown around online can scar a teenager's mind. The online world can be a ruthless arena where offensive comments, shaming, and demeaning behaviors run rampant. The psychological damage inflicted by these experiences can be profound and long-lasting.

The disruption of sleep due to social media use is another alarming concern. Our teens, captivated by the continuous online updates, are losing precious sleep. This loss is more than just a couple of groggy mornings; it's about hormonal imbalances, mood swings, decreased academic performance, and increased susceptibility to health problems.

Then, there's FOMO, or 'Fear of Missing Out,' not a modern-day phenomenon but one fuelled by social media. The constant need to stay connected, to keep up with every update or text thread, or to be at that party everyone is talking about is causing our children undue stress and anxiety, infringing upon any calm they may strive to achieve in their busy lives.

I want to underscore the severity of these impacts. I have a third try with my youngest, as I fully admit that I don't believe I got it right with either of my teenagers, Ted and Nina. We were navigating an explosion of social media, and I think it is only now that we can see the damaging effects that it has had over these last 10-15 years. I have signed the Wait Till 8th Pledge (see in the Resources section) and will attempt to keep my youngest child off social media until they are 18. When I finally succumbed to my middle daughter getting TikTok at the age of 13, I honestly believe that I saw the decline in her mental health before my eyes. She withdrew to her room, and before this terrible experiment had lasted two months, she was hurting herself. She also unwittingly made a wrong choice with a friend who was experiencing the grief of loss while being caught up in mental health content. Bad decisions were made, and damage was done. Our children's wellbeing is at stake here. We likely can't realistically entirely extricate social media from our teen's life. However, I will try with Tess, with a growing body of like-minded parents - it will be trying as it's so integrated into the fabric of their social interactions. So, where does that leave us as concerned parents?

The answer lies in active intervention and guidance. It's crucial not only to arm our teenagers with the knowledge to navigate this digital world but also to provide them with practical tools and guidelines. They also need to know about these recent reports about the damage it is doing. Arm them with the knowledge to begin making better choices on their own. With their brains' reward circuits already in overdrive, teenagers are particularly susceptible to the immediate gratification social media platforms can provide. The simple act of receiving a like or a positive comment can trigger a release of dopamine, the same 'feel-good' neurotransmitter associated with face-to-face social interactions and rewards. In a sense, social media can tap into the same neurological pathways as real-world social interactions.

Here are some basic essential strategies I suggest implementing.

Set Boundaries

One of the simplest yet most effective strategies is setting daily or weekly **time limits** for device and social media use. Apps like Screen Time on iOS or Digital Wellbeing on Android can monitor and control online time. As your teen gets older, you can continue to discuss and set limits together, but you could give them the power to override them if they are showing responsibility and working at lessening their screen time. It gives them control but pause for thought when they realize a limit has been reached. Teaching them to be mindful of screen time will be very helpful going forward. Any conversation regarding devices and screen time will probably cause tension, rolling of eyes or even rudeness, but I encourage you to persevere here.

Make sure, in settings, that any **app** your teen wants to get has to be **approved by you**. Again, this can be altered as age and responsibility allow; it may be different for each of your children if you have more than one.

As my daughter does regularly, encourage your teen to **delete the social media apps from their phone**, even suggest a trial, especially if they are finding them overwhelming or you see anxiety and stress increasing. It can be a potent tool for them to take a break like that.

Make sure to discuss that when they post, they have **like counts turned off**; it is a divisive and distasteful tool, again devised to addict our teens to more and more 'likes.'

Make sure that they remember that **anything they post will remain searchable and can affect their reputation**. They must not bully, humiliate, or upset anyone by spreading gossip or rumors.

Monitor Content

Stay updated on the types of content your teens are consuming and sharing. Privacy settings should be adjusted to restrict who can see their posts, and parental controls must be employed to filter out inappropriate material.

Encourage Offline Activities

Balance is key. Encourage your teens to participate in offline activities that they enjoy, whether it's sports, arts and crafts, or spending time with family and friends. This helps to diversify their experiences, so they do not become overly dependent on digital interactions.

Encourage Open Dialogue

Check-in with them. Create an environment where your teen feels comfortable discussing their social media usage, including any negative experiences like cyberbullying or peer pressure or even when they have made a mistake. Again, make sure they know the addictive possibilities. Consider, as a family, making a reasonable plan/contract between you all around online activities and screen time to maintain an open dialogue about this issue and to adapt as necessary. Even writing down the basic family rules around social media and device use can be powerful. I have included a basic plan in the References/Resources section at the end of the book.

Educate on Cybersecurity

Teach your teens the basics of cybersecurity, like the importance of strong passwords and the risks of sharing personal information online. Keep accounts private and be aware when certain games allow interactions with those unknown to them, especially if there is a chat feature.

Practice Active Listening

Be attentive to your teen's concerns about social media and its effects. Sometimes, they may want a listening ear more than immediate solutions.

By implementing these practical steps, our goal is to shield our teens from the potential harms of social media. This ensures they can enjoy its benefits without compromising their wellbeing.

Encouraging Mindfulness and Stress Management Techniques

The teenage years can be exciting, with new experiences and changes. However, they also come with their fair share of pressures and stressors. Academic pressure, social expectations, hormonal changes, and an increasing desire for independence can all contribute to a sense of unease and anxiety in teenagers. As a parent, your role in helping your teen navigate these stressors is essential.

One of the most effective tools at your disposal is mindfulness, which involves being fully present and engaged in the current moment. Teaching your teens to pay attention to their thoughts and feelings without judgment, you help them develop a valuable skill to manage stress and anxiety.

Recognizing the signs of stress in your teen is the first step towards helping them manage it. Changes in behavior, mood swings, sleep or appetite, difficulty concentrating, and feelings of constant worry are potential stress indicators.

Stress management involves equipping teens with the skills to handle stressors healthily and productively. Mindfulness, for one, is a practice that fosters a sense of calm and focus. It trains the mind to stay present, to tune into what's happening in the here and now, rather than getting lost in worries about the past or the future.

Here are three mindful practices that can benefit teens. Again, I cannot stress enough that phones must be out of the room for this or on 'do not disturb' or turned off (unless they are using a mindfulness app on their phone). I encourage parents to try these techniques, too!

Deep Breathing: A simple yet powerful technique that can help calm the mind. It involves taking slow, deep breaths and paying attention to each inhale and exhale. In through the nose, out through the mouth. The first few breaths can involve an audible sigh as you release your body›s tension. This technique can be beneficial during moments of high stress or anxiety.

Journaling: Encourage your teen to write down their thoughts and feelings. This practice provides a healthy outlet for emotions and helps foster self-awareness.

Body Scan Meditation: Start by finding a comfortable sitting or lying position in a quiet space. Then, gradually focus attention on different parts of the body, starting from the toes and moving slowly up to the head. It's a great way to encourage relaxation and presence.

Several apps provide meditation, yoga, and mindfulness lessons. These can also be very useful.

Chapter Takeaways

This chapter aimed to provide a comprehensive guide for parents on nurturing a healthy lifestyle for their teenagers. Here are the key takeaways:

Developing Healthy Eating Patterns

1. Nutrition Over Aesthetics: Focus on the nutritional value of food rather than weight loss or appearance.
2. Involve Your Teens: Make cooking and meal planning a shared activity to spark interest in healthy eating.
3. Educate: Provide educational resources and involve them in menu planning, grocery shopping, and cooking to make informed choices as time allows.

Developing Healthy Sleep Habits and Routines

1. Sleep is Non-Negotiable: Stress the importance of sleep for overall wellbeing.
2. Create a Sleep-Inducing Environment: A quiet, dark, and comfortable room can significantly improve sleep quality.
3. Limit Screen Time: Encourage putting away electronic devices at least an hour before bedtime.

Promoting Physical Health and Wellness

1. Find the Fun: Help your teen discover a physical activity they enjoy ensuring they stick with it.
2. Be a Role Model: Lead by example by maintaining an active lifestyle.
3. Start Small: If your teen is not used to physical activity, encourage them to start with small, achievable goals.

The Impact of Social Media on Teenagers' Lives

1. Set Boundaries: Limit the time spent on social media and stay updated on the types of content they interact with.
2. Open Communication: Create a safe space for discussing online experiences, challenges, and concerns.
3. Balance Digital and Real Life: Encourage participation in offline activities to balance their online presence.

Encouraging Mindfulness and Stress Management Techniques

1. Teach Mindfulness: Encourage deep breathing, journaling, and body scan meditation.
2. Be Aware of Stress Indicators: Mood swings, sleep changes, and behavioral shifts can be signs of stress.
3. Empower, Don't Enforce: Guide your teens to make wise decisions rather than forcing choices upon them.

CHAPTER 4
Building Strong Bonds: Steps to a Stronger Family

Every family encounter challenges and triumphs. The bonds forged between family members play a pivotal role in weathering these experiences. To strengthen these ties, here are our seven steps as a reminder:

Practice Active Listening: It's not just about hearing words but understanding the emotions behind them. This fosters a deeper connection and ensures every family member feels valued and understood.

Establish Trust: This becomes the foundation for a secure family environment. Trust ensures that each family member feels safe to express their feelings and concerns.

Bolster Self-Esteem and Encouragement: Recognize achievements and efforts. This positive reinforcement motivates and instills confidence.

Set Boundaries: Clearly define what's acceptable and what's not. This helps prevent misunderstandings and conflicts.

Practice Emotional Intelligence and be a Positive Role Model: By demonstrating emotional understanding and self-control, parents can guide their children in managing their emotions.

Encourage Open Dialogue: Promote an environment where family members can share their thoughts and concerns without fear of judgment.

Maintain Connection: Spend quality time together. This could be through family dinners, game nights, or other bonding activities.

Today's fast-paced world challenges the balance between work and family life. Striking this balance benefits the parents and children, teaching them responsibility and time management. Additionally, harmony in this balance positively influences the dynamics between siblings, fostering understanding, appreciation, and strong bonding.

During significant family changes, such as divorce, these bonds are tested. It's crucial to support teens through these transitions by actively listening, validating their feelings, and guiding them empathetically. Remember, a united family can withstand anything when grounded in understanding, empathy, and support.

Balancing Work and Family Life: Finding Harmony in a Busy World

As parents, we often juggle numerous roles. We work, manage households, care for our children, and try to maintain our relationships and personal wellbeing. It's easy to get overwhelmed, especially when your family includes teenagers navigating through their own changes and challenges. The key to managing this busy world is finding harmony between work and family.

When I was working as a medical doctor, the demands were intense. Long hours, emergency calls, and high-stress situations were all part of the job. I soon realized the importance of balancing and not letting my professional responsibilities consume me entirely. My family needed their mother, and I needed to be there for them.

In finding that balance, or at least a better balance in our lives, I discovered that it was crucial to slow down and assess my priorities. Work was important, but so was my family, health, and wellbeing. The tasks that could wait did wait, and those that were urgent or valuable got my attention. Delegation within the household was vital, and I found some relief in sharing responsibilities at work and home.

To this day, one of my biggest guiding principles is not sweating the small stuff. The unwashed dishes, the toys strewn around the living room, the missed deadline – it's not the end of the world to leave them a little longer. It's surprising how liberating it is when we realize not every battle is worth fighting and not every task is worth stressing over. I still don't do this well sometimes; I'm the first to admit that, but I keep trying. Certainly, as a parent, one of those great pieces of advice, 'pick your battles,' has remained with me ever since my son would struggle every time I would try and clothe him in a warm jacket when we were about to go out in the freezing cold in London. It would be a battle every time. My husband said, wait till he gets outside; he'll soon see how cold it is. What great advice! The battles stopped, and the jacket was hastily put on out in the cold, but he had that control and choice over the situation, even at that young age.

One piece of advice I strongly recommend to other parents is nurturing oneself. As parents, it's all too easy to neglect our own needs and self-care in the hustle and bustle of daily life, as focused as we are on taking care of our families. The truth is, however, that we can't effectively care for our loved ones if we're running on empty ourselves. The analogy of being unable to pour from an empty cup is more than just a cliché; it's a reality many of us face.

So, what does self-care look like? It doesn't have to be complicated or time-consuming. It can be as simple as taking a brisk 30-minute walk to clear your mind, diving into a novel that you've been eager to read but never found the time for, catching a game of tennis with a friend, or even indulging in a quiet cup of coffee in the solitude of your kitchen. These moments of "me time" are not just breaks from routine; they are essential refueling stops that recharge your emotional and physical batteries. When you take time to care for yourself, you're not just doing it for your own wellbeing—you're also indirectly benefiting your family by becoming a more patient, focused, and loving parent. For me, it's tennis, yoga, reading, or having a quiet cup of tea somewhere. My son recently, at 19, came home for a spell that wasn't planned. Finding these times was more challenging, and I know it affected my mood. Try to build it in; even 5 minutes of connecting to your breath in the bathroom is better than nothing!

Don't underestimate the power of self-care. It's not a luxury; it's a necessity. Investing in yourself is, in essence, investing in the wellbeing of your family. Take the time to recharge; you'll be surprised at how much more you can give when you do.

This brings me to another critical aspect - setting boundaries. It's essential to create clear lines between work and family time. When I am with my children, I try to make sure I am truly present, not just physically but mentally, too. I put the phone aside and keep work-related calls and emails to a minimum during that time.

Does it always work out perfectly? No. There will be days when the balance seems impossible, when work pressures ramp up or when family crises arise, or when just coordinating the family schedule keeps you on your device sending messages here and there. But that's okay. Accepting that imbalance is sometimes unavoidable and knowing it's temporary can take the pressure off. But explaining and sharing that with your child is often really valuable. My youngest daughter Tess will sometimes say, 'Why are you on your phone?' or worse, look at me in a resigned way when I pick up a call. Explaining what it is, if it is indeed an essential call to take in that moment, will at least help them understand even though it has invaded their time and space with you.

Regarding family dynamics, including teenagers in household chores and responsibilities is really important. These tasks are not connected to money; they are part of being a family. My children help with cleaning, cooking, and other chores. It's a way of instilling a sense of responsibility in them. And if you have younger children, make sure to start early. We made that mistake with our son Ted, and it made it hard for him ever to accept that this was just something he was required to do, leading to many battles. Be clear and consistent, and don't take no for an answer, even when it causes conflict. They will eventually get it!

We discovered that volunteering at a local homeless shelter's kitchen was a meaningful way to strengthen our family bonds while fulfilling our responsibilities to the community. By preparing and serving meals together, they not only learned valuable (bulk) cooking skills, but it also instilled a sense of compassion and empathy in all of us. Use the internet to find volunteer opportunities in your area- it can become a meaningful family activity.

Navigating through family dynamics and changes can be a challenging journey for teens. To provide the best support, we should strive to listen without judgment, validate their feelings, demonstrate open communication, and offer a consistent and stable environment. It's about being there, being available, and being supportive. Our older two, Ted and Nina, had ongoing conflicts when they were younger. Ted made life difficult for Nina, was often rough with her, and often not kind to her with his words. This made home, at times, quite a stressful and challenging place to be for quite a while. Keeping open lines of communication, getting help where necessary, and keeping our bonds strong with family activities were essential for our family during this time and beyond.

Ultimately, balancing work and family life isn't about achieving an elusive 'perfect' balance but finding what works for your family. It's about making conscious decisions about what's important, setting boundaries, and caring for yourself so you can care for the ones you love. And remember, it's a learning process, one that's constantly evolving, just like our children. So give yourself the grace and flexibility to adjust as needed, and know you're doing your best.

Sibling Dynamics and Conflict Resolution

The echo of laughter, the occasional clash of words, the shared secrets, and the companionship — the sibling dynamic is complex yet enriching. As a parent, navigating the rough waters of sibling rivalry and dynamics can be challenging and an opportunity to foster deeper bonds between your children.

"What is sibling rivalry?" you might ask. It is the inevitable discord that arises between siblings — be it out of competition, jealousy, or differences in personality and interests. From whom gets the last slice of pizza to who had the more fancy birthday cake to who gets to roll the dice first, these little skirmishes are a part of growing up with siblings.

The cause of such rivalries can be attributed to several factors, including each child's quest for individuality, their shared craving for parental attention, or their struggle with the uneven distribution of responsibilities or privileges.

Now, to manage these conflicts, it's crucial to remain impartial. The minute a parent takes sides, it fuels the fire of rivalry. As parents, we must promote open communication between our children, encouraging them to voice their thoughts and feelings. As I mentioned earlier, we had difficulties with Ted and Nina; navigating it was difficult, and we didn't always get it right. Don't ever think as parents that we aren't going to make mistakes on this journey; we all will.

Setting clear family rules can help establish order and fairness. Rules like respecting each other's space, knocking before entering bedrooms, taking turns, choosing kindness, and resolving disagreements are essential. And while the rules govern behavior, it's the family values that guide their spirit. Emphasizing values like empathy, kindness, and respect for others helps them build a supportive relationship over time.

But rules and values are not enough. It's important to model healthy conflict resolution. By doing this, we show our children how to negotiate, compromise, and solve problems fairly and respectfully. Making sure to have regular family dinners where debate skills and respectful listening are practiced is essential. Even when you go through a spell of challenging dinners, please don't give up. These skills must be practiced; this is the perfect place to do it.

Teaching them calming strategies, like deep breathing or counting to ten, can prevent heated moments from spiraling out of control. Assertiveness empowers them to express their feelings and stand up for themselves without aggression. However, taking a step or a beat and remaining respectful are all important techniques to learn in conflict resolution.

Supporting Your Teen Through Divorce and Family Changes

Divorce and family changes are another challenging aspect of family dynamics, particularly for teenagers. The world they knew is changing and, as parents, our role is to guide and support them through this transition.

Maintain open lines of communication, however painful and challenging it is, listening to their concerns and questions. Their feelings should be validated with empathy, and it's crucial to involve them in activities that distract and engage them, allowing them to process their emotions in a positive environment.

It is essential to watch out for signs that your teen might be struggling with the changes. If they show risky behaviors or significant changes in mood, appetite, or social interactions, or even pre-empting those things, it is worth seeking extra help. Don't shy away from involving a professional if you have the resources or access a therapist or school counselor. They most likely will need space to talk about the situation. I recommend this- talking to an impartial person outside the home is incredibly valuable in these situations, and I encourage you to instigate it sooner rather than later.

Teens, although nearing adulthood, are not adults yet. They experience emotions differently and often more intensely due to the physical and hormonal changes they are undergoing. It's essential to remember this when helping them adjust to divorce.

Opening up, sharing their fears, and expressing their emotions can be challenging for many teens. Parents must foster a safe environment where their teens feel comfortable voicing their concerns and questions. Patience is critical here as they may need time to express their feelings fully.

Validating their feelings is an important step. Show empathy, acknowledge their emotions, and reassure them that it's okay to feel like they do. They need to know that their feelings are valid and normal. As parents, it's crucial not to dismiss their feelings or rush them through processing the situation.

Active listening is crucial here. Engage in open, honest discussions about the changes happening. Ensure they understand that the divorce is not their fault and neither parent loves them any less because of it. This may need repeating and repeating. There could also be anger towards you or your spouse, and however hard that is to bear, you need to be there for them, whatever the emotions they express.

As a co-parent, maintaining consistency and unity in decisions concerning your teen's upbringing can offer stability in their lives. They need to see that while the marital relationship is ending, the parental relationship continues, and their wellbeing remains a priority.

Encourage involvement in activities they enjoy. This can help them manage stress, express themselves, and maintain a sense of normalcy amidst the changes. It can range from sports and art to spending time with friends.

Signs that a teenager is struggling with the changes might include:

- A change in their behavior.
- Withdrawal from social activities.
- Decline in academic performance.
- Exhibiting risky behaviors.

If noticed, consider seeking professional help. Therapists, counselors, or support groups can provide additional resources to help them cope.

However, it's essential to remember that not all teens react the same way to divorce. Some might display overt signs of distress, while others might internalize their feelings. Some might adapt quickly, while others might take more time to adjust.

Remember, helping a teen through divorce and family changes doesn't end with addressing immediate reactions. It's a journey that involves ongoing conversation, reassurance, and support. Being patient, understanding, and open during this challenging transition can help your teen cope more effectively. They can learn valuable lessons about resilience, adaptability, and handling life's inevitable changes, which will serve them well into adulthood.

One of Nina's friends was so frustrated; I think 'mad' was the term she used with her divorced parents for not communicating better. She wished they had understood that their conflicts and inconsistent rules caused her stress and confusion.

Every action or inaction echoes within the family dynamics, particularly impacting teenagers in a delicate phase of their own lives.

Balancing family dynamics is a continuous process of adjusting and adapting, understanding and empathy, patience, and communication. We have also seen the role of routines and the necessity to keep sight of the individual needs of each family member. Whether dealing with divorce, sibling conflict, or the pressures of work-life balance, the key lies in maintaining open lines of communication, setting clear boundaries, and offering consistent and compassionate support.

Chapter Takeaways

1. The Importance of Family Bonds: The strength of a family is rooted in the bonds forged between its members. These bonds become even more crucial when the family goes through challenges such as divorce or significant life changes.

2. Work-Family Life Balance: Striking a balance between professional responsibilities and family time is essential for fostering a harmonious and supportive environment at home. It's not just about you; it teaches your children valuable life skills like responsibility and time management.

3. Self-Care is Family Care: Taking time to focus on your wellbeing isn't selfish; it's a necessary aspect of being an effective parent. You can't pour from an empty cup; your emotional and physical health directly impacts your family.

4. Sibling Dynamics: Sibling relationships can be a source of both conflict and support. The role of parents in managing sibling conflict is to remain impartial and foster open communication and fair rules, all while teaching conflict resolution skills.

5. Support During Family Changes: Significant family changes, like divorce, can be tough on teens. The keys to helping them through these times are open communication, validating their feelings, and consistent parenting.

6. Setting Boundaries: Creating clear lines between work and family time helps in being truly present for your family. This also helps in setting expectations for your family and work colleagues.

7. Involvement in Household Responsibilities: Including teenagers in household chores instills a

sense of responsibility and offers a way to spend quality time together as a family.

8. Community Service: Activities like volunteering can serve as an excellent way for families to spend time together while teaching valuable life skills and instilling a sense of empathy and compassion.

9. Professional Help: Don't hesitate to seek professional advice if you notice signs of struggle in your teen's behavior, especially during challenging times like a divorce.

10. It's a Continuous Process: Balancing work, family life, and individual needs is a dynamic, ongoing process. Flexibility, communication, and empathy are crucial to navigating the ever-changing needs and challenges that come your way.

CHAPTER 5

Navigating Challenges in Your Teens' Mental Health

I have laid down the seven essential strategies for success in communicating with our teens and discussed teenage brain development. We have also discussed how to help our teens develop as healthy a lifestyle as possible and how we can create a healthy family environment for them. Despite these measures and ideas being implemented, things can go wrong, and sometimes seriously wrong. This chapter aims to give you a broad overview of some of the mental health challenges we can see in our teens.

As the mother of two teenagers and an 11-year-old, I have had my fair share of parenting experiences, and that includes mental health challenges. It's what compelled me to write this book, sharing some of the knowledge I gleaned as a doctor looking after teens in the family health care setting and our personal experiences. It's tough, and I'm continually learning from it. There are some resources at the back of the book and links to the facts and figures mentioned in this chapter.

Recent data from the Centers for Disease Control and Prevention (CDC) paints a stark picture of mental health challenges in our teenagers: The prevalence of mental health issues among teenagers is on the rise and has been rising steadily since social media took off 10-15 years ago, with a further significant increase during the pandemic. The CDC reports that the percentage of children aged 3-17 years who have been diagnosed with either anxiety or depression has increased from 5.4% in 2003 to 8.4% in 2012. In 2023, 11.5% of teenagers have been diagnosed with severe major depressive disorder. It's a pretty shocking statistic.

But why are these figures so high, and why are they continuing to rise? Experts suggest that increased pressure at school, cyberbullying, exposure to traumatic events (such as the pandemic) and changing family dynamics are all contributing factors. I know I keep talking about this, but the pervasive influence of social media can amplify these stresses, offering both a platform for cyberbullying and a space where unrealistic expectations can be set. I mentioned earlier that I finally let my daughter Nina have TikTok at 13 and literally saw before my eyes a change in her mental health. Studies show that repeated checking of social media around the age of 12/13 leads to changes in the brain over three years, causing teens to become more sensitive to social feedback.

The issue here isn't that parents are ill-equipped to handle situations that arise with their teens. Certainly, no parenting is perfect. It's more about a generation dealing with new pressures and expectations that are often difficult to comprehend and handle. With the ultra-connectedness of our youth, new challenges complicate their whole existence, which we did not have to contend with ourselves at that age. We are navigating a whole new uncharted era. Don't forget the horrific fact that social media has been designed to addict and influence our teens in a pervasive way. That's why in 2023, as I write this book, an unprecedented federal lawsuit was filed by 33 attorneys general, alleging that Meta's (formally Facebook's) products have harmed minors and contributed to the mental health crisis in the United States.

While you read this chapter, keep the seven strategies from Chapter 1 in mind, and keep empathy at the forefront of your mind whether you are navigating these issues or not.

This chapter is not going to be fully comprehensive as this would take the whole book and beyond, but it will explore some of the most common mental health challenges teenagers face, such as anxiety, depression, and eating disorders. As a parent, you may have questioned - How do I know if my teen is struggling? What signs should I be aware of? What mental health conditions are most common in teenagers? This chapter will answer these questions, equipping you with knowledge and tools to proactively promote your teen's mental health. As a mother, mental health challenges have been a personal journey for me, and I want to address them in the most straightforward way possible so that, in the future, you can recognize warning signs and seek the help that your family needs.

I watched as Nina withdrew into her room more and more, her happier disposition fading into a disquieting silence. She used to be so energetic and now seemed overshadowed by a cloud of heaviness and uncertainty. Did her recent bout of COVID-19 cause this, or was this a sign of something more severe and deep-seated? I told her I'd noticed that she seemed to be struggling and becoming far less social and more withdrawn. She let her guard down one day, and I recognized the subtle signs of social anxiety and depression in her. I knew deep down we had a problem, but it needed a moment where she felt she could be actively listened to and have the time and space to open up for it to all come pouring out. It was a pivotal moment, and it was the beginning of a long road of illness and slow recovery that became our family's shared journey. I know life is full of pressures, time constraints, and even our addictions to electronics, but finding moments like these can be clarifying and so important for your relationship with your teen.

Adolescent Mental Health & Anxiety: Recognizing and Addressing Concerns

As we've discussed, adolescence is a critical developmental stage marked by significant physical, emotional, and social changes. Amidst these changes, adolescents are frequently faced with new challenges and pressures that can affect their mental wellbeing. The World Health Organization (WHO) states that half of all mental health conditions start by 14 years of age, but most cases are undetected and untreated at this early stage. The CDC released figures in 2021 showing that over 12 months, 18.9% of teens reported any mental health treatment.

Sadly, suicide rates among teenagers have been on an upward trend. A CDC study revealed that the suicide rate for young people aged 10-24 increased by 56% between 2007 and 2017. The most significant annual increase in suicide occurred from 2016 to 2017, a 10% increase from 9.6 to 10.6 per 100,000. I'm afraid the statistics don't get any better in this area; they are gradually worsening, and we must stay vigilant.

As parents, it really can sometimes be hard to differentiate between typical teenage angst and signs of a mental health disorder. Our teens might not consistently articulate their feelings, making it even more difficult for parents to understand what they're going through. However, there are specific indicators you can watch out for. These may include changes in behavior, like withdrawal from activities or people they once enjoyed, drastic changes in weight or appearance, eating pattern changes, difficulty concentrating, or feelings of hopelessness or worthlessness. And believe me, the sooner you seek help or consultation, the better. Even if it turns out to be in the normal range, your teen will appreciate your care and concern, and if it is a significant problem, then earlier treatment and support are always better. Use the steps I've outlined to actively listen and give your teen space to express their struggles.

Here, I am sharing with you the most common mental health disorders among adolescents so that you can recognize possible problems with your teen, keep an eye out for changes in their behavior, and seek help or advice where necessary:

Anxiety Disorders

These are one of the most common mental health concerns among adolescents, affecting nearly 31.9% of teenagers aged 13-18, according to the National Institute of Mental Health. Cases have doubled globally since the pandemic, according to recent studies.

Adolescents with anxiety may experience excessive and persistent fear, restlessness, irritability, panic attacks, and difficulty sleeping and concentrating. Anxiety disorders often interfere with daily activities, as your child may go to great lengths to avoid the objects or situations that trigger these feelings. If left unaddressed, anxiety can lead to more severe mental health issues, including depression and suicide.

Cognitive-behavioral therapy (CBT), a type of talking therapy that challenges unhelpful/anxiety-making thoughts and teaches self-help strategies to deal with them in the moment, is an excellent first mode of treatment for anxiety disorders. Anxiety disorders can also be treated using DBT (Dialectical Behaviour Therapy), typically a longer-form treatment than CBT. This type of treatment promotes acceptance of negative emotions/anxieties, feeling them and letting them go. Medications may be needed at some point and include antidepressants like SSRIs (selective serotonin reuptake inhibitors), some of which are particularly good for treating anxiety, and also beta-blockers, such as propranolol, can play a role in helping with the physical symptoms of anxiety.

Depressive Disorders

In teens, these tend to take one of three forms:

Firstly, **Major Depressive Disorder** (often known as clinical depression) is a severe form of depression and one of the most common mental disorders affecting teens. Major Depressive Disorder is characterized by persistent (at least two weeks) low mood, feelings of sadness, hopelessness, and a lack of interest, and sometimes complete inability to participate in normal daily activities, such as working, studying, sleeping, and eating. Symptoms include:

- Fatigue and loss of energy
- Difficulty concentrating
- Changes in sleep patterns (insomnia or excessive sleepiness)
- Appetite changes and weight fluctuations
- Feelings of guilt or worthlessness
- Suicidal thoughts or tendencies

Secondly, **Bipolar Disorder** involves episodes of mood swings ranging from depressive lows to manic highs, which can both last for weeks. The symptoms during these phases can vary significantly:

- Manic Phase: Elevated mood, increased energy, decreased need for sleep, grandiosity, and impulsivity.
- Depressive Phase: Low mood, lack of energy, feelings of hopelessness, and disinterest in activities once enjoyed.

And thirdly, **Persistent Depressive Disorder** (also known as dysthymia). A child has to have had a persistent low/sad mood for at least 12 months to be diagnosed. They may also have had Major Depressive episodes within that time.

It's essential to be aware that depression will affect a child's body, mind, and thoughts. This type of mood disorder can't just be willed away. It can affect your child's sleeping, eating habits, and thought processes and take a toll on the family.

Our daughter Nina was diagnosed with depression and is now on treatment with medication and therapy. Some days, it is the most painful thing to watch your baby suffering that kind of mental pain and anguish, sometimes wishing they weren't even alive. Excruciating, in fact. Somehow, we get up and carry on; the anguish doesn't go away, but use your supports and check in regularly with your teen and yourself.

As far as causes for this problem, it is usually hard to pinpoint and can be related to several factors. There can be genetic factors, particularly if a parent or close family member has had depression when young, brain chemistry (when certain neurotransmitters in your brain are unbalanced or abnormal), hormone level changes, stress, abuse, neglect, physical/emotional trauma, loss of someone close, loss of a relationship and other developmental/learning problems can contribute.

Treatment usually involves a combination of talk therapy, and even in children, medications, such as antidepressants, can be very helpful. A note on this: work with your family doctor or school to find a way for your teen to work with a therapist if possible. If it doesn't seem to be working with one counselor/therapist, see if you can find an alternative.

Eating Disorders

Eating disorders are an increasingly recognized mental health issue among adolescents. The National Institute of Mental Health (NIMH) reports that about 2.7% of teens aged 13-18 have struggled with an eating disorder at some point in their lives. Alarmingly, despite the severity of these disorders, less than a third of people with eating disorders receive treatment. A 2021 study published in the Journal of Adolescent Health reported a significant increase in eating disorders among adolescents in several different countries over the past decade. This upsurge is believed to be associated with a variety of factors, including societal beauty standards, increased exposure to media, and the stress and isolation induced by the COVID-19 pandemic.

Misunderstandings about eating disorders are rife. Many believe they stem from vanity or a bid for attention. However, eating disorders are typically driven by deep-rooted, underlying issues often tied to feelings of control, self-esteem, and self-perception. They're not about wanting to look a certain way but are complex disorders with both psychological and physical implications.

These disorders are not discriminatory; they affect adolescents irrespective of gender, age, ethnicity, and socioeconomic status. The causes of eating disorders are diverse, often a mix of genetic, psychological, and sociocultural factors. They can stem from a family history of eating disorders, dieting, body dissatisfaction, or stressful transitions, but the underlying cause is usually rooted in a deeper psychological trauma or issue. On a broader scale, societal pressure to conform to specific beauty standards can contribute to these disorders. However, certain factors increase the risk. For example, females are more likely to develop an eating disorder than males, although the incidence in males is growing. Teens who have a family member with an eating disorder are also at higher risk. According to the American Academy of Child & Adolescent Psychiatry, teens who have a parent or sibling with an eating disorder are up to 11 times more likely to develop the disorder themselves.

Furthermore, certain personality traits such as perfectionism and obsessiveness have been associated with a higher risk of developing an eating disorder. It is also important to note that eating disorders are often associated with diagnoses of anxiety and depression. If these are poorly treated, it is much harder to treat the eating disorder.

Classifications of the main Eating Disorders:

Anorexia nervosa/Atypical Anorexia nervosa-huge weight loss driven by an intense fear of gaining weight or becoming fat. In atypical Anorexia, despite weight remaining in the normal range for height, there has been huge weight loss, as in Anorexia. Symptoms and signs vary, but some warning signs include preoccupation with weight, food, dieting, or body size, drastic weight changes, negative self-talk about body image, intense fear of weight gain, distorted perceptions of body image, and avoidance of meals. Do not assume that someone who does not look 'underweight' does not have an eating disorder; this is a myth; someone with what would be considered 'normal weight' or even 'obese' can have Anorexia or Bulimia. In severe cases, you may notice signs of malnutrition, like fainting, hair loss, or extreme fatigue.

Bulimia -characterized by alternate dieting or eating low-calorie 'safe' foods with binge-eating on high-calorie 'forbidden' foods. Binge eating involves eating large amounts of food in a short period of time and is associated with feelings of shame and embarrassment. In this disease, binge behavior will happen at least weekly and then be followed by weight-reducing behaviors such as laxative use, vomiting, fasting, or compulsive exercising. As with Anorexia, those with Bulimia are preoccupied with thoughts of food, weight, and shape, which negatively impact their feelings of worth.

Binge-eating disorder-binge eating episodes occur at least every week but are not regularly followed by compensatory measures.

Avoidant Restrictive Food Intake Disorder (ARFID)- a newer diagnosis involving a consistent lack of meeting nutritional needs involving restricting intake and picky eating.

Among mental health disorders, eating disorders have the highest mortality rate, which underscores the severity and grave nature of these conditions. Despite their prevalence and deadly potential, they can receive less attention and resources compared to other mental health disorders, making it all the more crucial for parents to be informed and vigilant about the signs and potential risks associated with them, and is partly why I have given them so much attention in this book. I let my daughter start skipping breakfast (terrible idea, using hindsight), but it was only when I realized some months later that I had not renewed money on her school card for lunch that it clicked we were dealing with restriction in the extreme. Also, with hindsight, allowing her to become a vegetarian three years earlier might not have been the best idea. If I had realized how that small 'win' to control would have such implications on her diet and intake later on, possibly masking a greater need for control, I might have actively discouraged this path, whereas, at the time, I wanted to support her moral objection.

One of the most challenging parts of dealing with eating disorders, or any other mental health condition, is accepting the need for professional help. As parents, we strive to provide the best for our children and to protect them, and it can be hard to admit that they may need assistance beyond what we can provide. If you notice persistent unhealthy eating habits or extreme behavior related to food or body image, reach out to your doctor; don't wait.

I won't lie; the eating disorder journey we took with Nina has been one of the toughest we've ever embarked on as a family. But it's also been one of growth, understanding, and deepening bonds. It has taught us the power of resilience, the importance of open communication, and the immense strength of unity. As we continue to support our daughter, we've seen her gradually reclaim her life from the clutches of this disorder, which literally, over time, reduces it to nothing.

It would need another book to tell you about the ins and outs of the treatment we undertook. There are several ways to go, including support from a psychotherapist, medical doctor, and dietician to intensive outpatient treatment centers, in-patient treatment, and now even intensive online programs. It needs a multidisciplinary approach, with each treatment plan being customized to meet the needs of the individual after a thorough evaluation. As I mentioned earlier, poorly treated anxiety and depression can severely hamper recovery. We went the family route, using a gold-standard treatment protocol called Family Based Treatment (FBT). It was grueling, but we came out the other side, using all the resources our family could muster, with the support of a family therapist (links to FBT in the Resources section). FBT is the 'cheapest' way to go, but it is the most intensive and hands-on for the family. Treatment centers can be prohibitively expensive but discuss with your family doctor to see what might work for your family.

In my family's journey, the singular truth that has consistently surfaced is the power of communication. I let that slip before we got a diagnosis; my eye was off the ball. A note about that: Don't beat yourself up about things like that; it can happen. We are all human and therefore fallible- it's not worth the energy. Deal with the situation as you find it and look forward, one step at a time, day by day. Open dialogue between us as parents and our daughter has been crucial and ultimately successful in beating this.

Attention Deficit Hyperactivity Disorder (ADHD)

This is one of the most common neurodevelopmental disorders of childhood that often lasts into adulthood. It is classed as a mental health disorder by the American Psychiatric Association. Adolescents with ADHD may have trouble paying attention (not being able to keep focus), hyperactivity, which manifests as excess movement not fitting to a particular setting, and impulsive behaviors, which are acts that occur in the moment without thought. There are three different types-predominantly inattention, predominantly hyperactive/impulsive, and the third type is a combination of both.

Treatment includes behavioral, ways to minimize distractions, increase structure and organization, study skills training, change in classroom setup, modified curriculum, and alternate learning techniques. This can be supported by medication in the form of psychostimulants when necessary.

Other Mental Health issues in teens

- Teen trauma and PTSD
- Teen Schizophrenia
- Obsessive-Compulsive Disorder (OCD)
- Personality Disorders including Borderline, Narcissistic, Dissociative, Histrionic,
- Dissociative Identity Disorder
- Disruptive Behavior Disorders (DBDs)

- Gaming Disorder-newly classified as a mental health condition, an addictive disorder related, in this case, to video gaming obsession.

This book cannot go into detail about all the mental health conditions out there that could affect your teen. Look out for changes in your teen, and make sure to carve out that time to check in with them so that you pick up on subtle things. The more you talk to them, the more comfortable they will feel about confiding in you, and the easier it will be to detect changes. Changes in school performance, excessive worry or anxiety, hyperactive behavior, persistent nightmares, and persistent disobedience or aggression are all things to think about and take a second look at. Make sure to maintain, as best you can, a supportive home environment that promotes a sense of safety and security for your teen.

Early detection and treatment play a crucial role in managing mental health disorders. Consult a mental health professional if you are in doubt. Don't delay seeking help, even if you feel some stigma. Educate yourself so that you are better informed-you've already started that by reading this book! It is better to ask questions and educate yourself than ignore symptoms and signs. Mental health disorders are treatable, and with the right help and support, your teen can overcome or at least be supported in these challenges and lead a fulfilling life.

Chapter Takeaways

1. Rising Prevalence of Mental Health Issues: The increasing rates of anxiety, depression, and other mental health issues among teens are alarming. Understanding the magnitude of the problem is the first step in addressing it.

2. Underlying Causes: Multiple factors contribute to the rise in mental health issues among teens, including academic pressures, cyberbullying, societal expectations, and significant life changes.

3. Early Detection is Crucial: Parents should be aware of the signs and symptoms of mental health disorders. These can include changes in behavior, academic performance, and social interactions. Early intervention can be critical in preventing the escalation of issues.

4. Open Communication: Fostering a home environment where open dialogue about feelings, challenges, and concerns is encouraged can significantly affect a teen's mental wellbeing.

5. Types of Disorders: Understanding the types of mental health disorders that commonly affect teenagers, such as anxiety disorders, mood disorders, ADHD, and eating disorders, can equip parents with the necessary knowledge to seek timely help.

6. Treatment Options: Most mental health conditions are treatable with a combination of medication and psychotherapy. Treatment is personalized and may require a multidisciplinary approach.

7. Role of Family: The family plays a pivotal role in the early detection, treatment, and ongoing support for teens dealing with mental health issues. Family involvement can range from sharing meals to seeking professional help as a unit.

8. Self-Care for Parents: Parents must also take time for their self-care. Dealing with a child's mental health issues can be draining, and a well-cared-for parent is better equipped to support their child.

9. Professional Help: Don't hesitate to seek professional guidance if you notice persistent changes in your teen's behavior or wellbeing. There's no substitute for expert advice and treatment.

10. Long-term Support: Supporting a teen with mental health issues is a long-term commitment that requires patience, understanding, and adaptability. It's a journey that the family undertakes together, and it can strengthen family bonds and personal growth for all involved.

CHAPTER 6

Setting Boundaries and Dealing with Substance Use, Addiction, and Other Risk-Taking Behaviors

As parents, we're constantly balancing our desire to protect our children with the need to let them learn from their own experiences. Dealing with potential substance use, addiction, and risk-taking behaviors can be overwhelming, but with the proper knowledge and tools, we can guide our children through this. Teens are going to experiment. What is more concerning is the possibility of them slipping into regular drug or alcohol use and possible dependence. I am not suggesting tackling this will be plain sailing. Don't forget to constantly review the seven steps in Chapter 1 while reading this book. Trusting your teen is crucial, as is giving them the tools they need to make good decisions. Remember, once they step over the line into bad decision-making in the context of some of these risky behaviors, trust is lost and needs to be earned back.

Substance use, including drugs, alcohol, and tobacco, is a concern that many parents face. The allure of these substances can be strong for teenagers, as they can promise a temporary escape from the pressures of adolescence. However, the consequences of substance use can be severe, affecting their health, safety, and future. As parents, understanding why teenagers are drawn to these substances and knowing the signs of use can help us intervene early.

In addition to substance use, teenagers are often drawn to risk-taking behaviors. This is a natural part of their development as they seek to assert their independence and test boundaries. However, some risks, such as unprotected sex, dangerous driving, illegal activities, fighting, and truancy, can have dire consequences. Understanding the reasons behind these behaviors and equipping ourselves with strategies to guide our teens toward safer choices is crucial.

In this chapter, we will delve into the complexities of substance use and risk-taking behaviors. Drawing from my own experiences as a mother and insights from my medical background, I aim to provide you with an understanding of these issues and practical strategies to address them. The journey won't always be smooth, but together, we can guide and even coax our teens to make wiser choices.

My son struggled socially in middle school. He had a keen desire to fit in and be part of a group, but he found the tools he needed hard to master, coupled with a tendency to seek out risky experiences. He ended up befriending a boy who did not influence him well. His friend was not supported at home, had little parental supervision, and took to drugs (marijuana) and encouraged Ted to go the same way. This was a battle zone from my point of view. I was not, under any circumstances, going to let my son go far down this road, and I fought it and him with all the strength I had, possibly to the detriment of my other children. My focus was 'saving' him from the clutches of regular marijuana use (and, of course, anything stronger, that slippery slope I was so afraid of). Before we delve into this further, it is essential to state that teenagers who are under severe stress or feeling isolated are more at risk of seeking out risky behavior.

Substance, Alcohol, and Smoking Use

Substances like drugs, alcohol, and tobacco often become points of concern as our children venture into their teenage years. We might find ourselves grappling with questions about how to approach these topics, how to identify warning signs, and, most importantly, how to guide our teens to make responsible choices. It's a lot to take in, but knowledge is (maybe not quite) half the battle. In the following sections, we'll thoroughly explore these substances and arm ourselves with practical knowledge.

Drugs

This is a genuine concern, particularly at those ubiquitous high school parties, and the earlier we understand it, the better we can equip ourselves and our teens to handle it. Here are some commonly used substances, but by no means an exhaustive list:

- Marijuana (cannabis)
- Prescription medications, especially painkillers and stimulants
- Synthetic cannabinoids, known as Spice or K2
- Inhalants, such as glue or aerosol sprays
- MDMA (Ecstasy or Molly)
- Cocaine and crack cocaine
- Methamphetamine
- LSD and other hallucinogens
- Heroin, Fentanyl, and other opiates

Why Teens Use Drugs

As we know from Chapter 2, the adolescent brain is still developing, making it more susceptible to the allure of experimentation and risk-taking. Some reasons teenagers might be drawn to drug use include:

- **Curiosity:** Many are curious about the effects these substances might have.
- **Peer pressure:** The desire to fit in can be a powerful motivator.

- **Stress relief:** Teens might turn to substances as a way to deal with stress, anxiety, or emotional pain.
- **Rebellion:** Some teenagers might use drugs as a way to rebel or to feel more ‹adult.›

Consequences, Health Effects, and Warning Signs

The health implications of drug use are far-reaching. Physically, there can be immediate impacts such as drowsiness, impaired judgment, and slower reflexes. Over time, drug use can lead to more severe consequences like liver damage, respiratory issues, and even addiction. The social and emotional impacts can be just as damaging, affecting relationships, academic performance, and mental health.

Here are some potential effects and consequences specific to various drugs (not an exhaustive list):

- **Marijuana:** Impaired short-term memory, concentration, and attention, altered judgment, coordination issues, bloodshot eyes, increased appetite, distorted perception, and persistent cough (if smoked).
- **Synthetic cannabinoids:** Agitation, confusion, hallucinations, anxiety, paranoia.
- **Prescription medications:** depends on which medication but can cause dependency, especially with painkillers, which can lead to overdoses or transitioning to more dangerous drugs like heroin.

- **Inhalants:** Chemical odors on clothing or breath, a runny nose, rashes, sores around the mouth or nose. Belligerence, apathy, impaired judgment, nausea, vomiting, confusion, and delirium at higher doses
- **Methamphetamine:** Agitation/aggression, hyperactivity, decreased appetite, blurred vision, confusion, chest pain or discomfort, change in consciousness
- **MDMA (Ecstasy or Molly):** Increased affection, heightened senses, reduced appetite, lack of need for sleep, panic attacks, faintness, increased blood pressure, loss of consciousness, and seizures in overdose.
- **Cocaine and Crack Cocaine:** Excitability, increased energy, dilated pupils, dizziness, abdominal pain, chills, fast heartbeat, hallucinations, confusion.
- **LSD and other Hallucinogens:** Dilated pupils, erratic behavior, detachment from surroundings, euphoria, confusion, trouble concentrating, headaches, nausea, vomiting, chills, possible hallucinations.
- **Heroin and other Opiates:** Slurred speech, constricted pupils, a slow gait, sedation, nausea, constipation, dizziness, respiratory depression.

Talking with Your Teen About Drugs

Open and honest communication is essential. Start the conversation early and aim for a two-way dialogue. Listen to their concerns and share your own. Drive home the risks involved and the impact that drug use can have on their lives.

Prevention

- Educate: Provide factual information about the dangers of drug use.
- Be Present: Spend quality time with your teen.
- Monitor: Know where your teen is and who they are with.
- Set Boundaries: Make your expectations clear.

Recognizing the signs of drug use early can make a significant difference. I spoke with my son about this recently, long after he had stopped taking drugs (marijuana). He confessed that I had never missed one of his drug-taking episodes. I would test him, usually just to confirm. He added that the testing was the one thing that stopped him in the end, and he was glad that's how I'd tackled it. He tried everything to get around me, even hiding bottles of urine from another day to present to me, but I was aware of the tricks and manipulations teens are capable of. We did not want this situation to escalate in a household with younger siblings. He ended up suddenly stopping, literally from one day to the next. This episode caused so much conflict and trust issues and was truly exhausting, but it was over. All good, you might say…well, that was until he started driving.

General Behavioral Signs:

- Declining academic performance or frequent absences from school.
- A change in friends or social groups.
- Loss of interest in previously enjoyed activities.
- Increased secrecy or a sudden demand for privacy.
- Borrowing money frequently or missing valuables.

How to Get Help

If you believe your teen is involved in substance use, however scary it is, try to approach the situation with understanding and care, offering support rather than punishment. The more you punish and argue, the more they will push back. Ultimately, you know your child the best, but use these strategies as a guide.

General Steps:

1. **Open a Dialogue:** Initiate a calm and non-confrontational conversation. Listen actively to what they have to say.

2. **Educate Yourself:** Understanding the substance they're using can better equip you to address the issue.

3. **Seek Professional Counsel:** A drug counselor or therapist can provide expert advice. Your school advisor or family doctor should be able to help with resources in your area.

Specific Drug-Related Interventions:

- **Marijuana:** Although viewed by many as less harmful, long-term use can lead to addiction. Consider counseling that specifically addresses marijuana use.
- **Prescription Medications:** Reach out to the prescribing doctor to discuss concerns. They can offer guidance on safely reducing and discontinuing the medication if needed.
- **Synthetic Cannabinoids (Spice or K2):** These can have unpredictable effects. Immediate medical attention might be required in acute cases.
- **Inhalants:** Given the potential immediate risk, consider seeking medical evaluation if you believe your teen is currently under the influence.
- **MDMA (Ecstasy or Molly):** Engage in group or individual therapy sessions that specifically address MDMA use.

- **Cocaine and Crack Cocaine:** Given their highly addictive nature, consider inpatient or outpatient rehab programs.
- **Methamphetamine:** As with cocaine, rehabilitation programs can be beneficial.
- **LSD and other Hallucinogens:** Engage in therapy that focuses on the psychological effects of hallucinogens.
- **Heroin and other Opiates:** Immediate medical intervention is crucial, followed by detox and rehabilitation.

Stay involved throughout the recovery process and try to stick to a plan. Your teen will need all the support they can get, and knowing they have a caring figure in their life can make all the difference.

A note about Fentanyl

I don't want to scare you too much, but this needs to be said. As I write, criminal drug networks are mass-producing fake pills that look and seem like prescription medication and falsely marketing them to the public. These are being sold on social media and e-commerce sites, but they often contain Fentanyl or methamphetamine. Particularly in the case of Fentanyl, one pill can kill you. There are resources online and in communities to train teens to deliver naloxone, the antidote drug to opiate poisoning (see websites in resources), which will help in certain situations, but warning and trying to prevent your teen from buying drugs online is a much safer approach. Have them do the training, too, so that they are aware of the warning signs of fentanyl poisoning. They could potentially save a life.

A note about US prescribing

Even after 16 years of living here, I am sad to say that I am still shocked by some prescribing practices employed here in the States. I know of cases of children being prescribed too many opiates after a sports injury operation, say, where the prescribing was not controlled. The prescriber needs to take responsibility to ensure there is no possibility of addiction, and this involves educating the family on potential dependence and limiting prescriptions. These drugs need to be incredibly carefully prescribed to adults and children alike-it is very easy to end up with bottles of oxycodone or other codeine-based medicines in any household, even after a simple procedure, where very few are ever warranted, and the dangers are not spelled out. Addiction can happen WITHIN A WEEK where opiates are concerned, and this includes codeine-based products. You only need to look at the statistics of opiate dependence and overdose in this country to see the bleak, stark facts of uncontrolled prescribing. Keep any prescribed drugs of your own in a safe place, and push back for a clear plan if you or your child is offered this medication. Safely dispose of any leftover prescribed medicines.

Alcohol

Alcohol is a substance that has been both celebrated and condemned throughout history. Its presence at social gatherings, family events, and cultural rituals makes it a common fixture in our lives. However, as a parent, the thought of my teenager being exposed to alcohol can evoke feelings of anxiety and concern, especially for teens like my daughter with a driving license.

Why Teens Drink

The reasons teens may be drawn to alcohol are multifaceted. Peer pressure can play a significant role, with many teens feeling the urge to fit in or avoid being labeled as "different." Additionally, the portrayal of alcohol in the media as a gateway to fun and relaxation can be enticing. Some teens may also view drinking as a way to rebel or seek a temporary escape from personal problems or stress. Some may see drinking as a culture in their own homes or families. This can also have an impact. I spoke to one couple who started having 'drinks before dinner' with their teens during the pandemic, which became quite the social event in their home. I would caution against this idea. The longer teens can avoid normalized and very regular social drinking, the better. Studies show that they then fare better in their long-term relationship with alcohol.

Consequences and Health Effects

While an occasional glass of wine or beer might seem harmless, the developing teenage brain is particularly susceptible to the effects of alcohol. Short-term effects can include impaired judgment, lack of coordination, and risky behavior. Repeated consumption can lead to long-term issues such as memory problems, liver disease, and even the development of an alcohol use disorder.

Also, regular alcohol use in teens has been linked to academic challenges, increased risk of physical and sexual assault, and even fatalities from accidents, suicides, or alcohol poisoning.

Talking with Your Teen About Alcohol

Initiating a dialogue about alcohol is crucial. Share facts about the potential dangers and repercussions of underage drinking. A non-confrontational approach can often lead to more open and honest discussions. Please encourage them to share their views and experiences related to alcohol and listen attentively. I'm sure you're thinking my son Ted indulged this way, judging by his risk-taking history, but this was one thing we did not have to worry about with him! My daughter Nina is more interested, so we are discussing it, and she has been honest when she has tried some at a party. She actually had a hangover the other day. This was the perfect segue into a discussion about alcohol and has given her a new perspective on it, as it ruined her weekend. It is unlikely and frankly unrealistic that your teen will get through their teenage years without being tempted. Work with them on the points below.

Prevention

- Education: Equip your teen with factual information about alcohol.
- Role Modeling: Lead by example. Your teen will often mirror your relationship with alcohol.
- Open Dialogue: Encourage questions and provide a safe space for discussion.
- Know Their Friends: Knowing your teen's social circle can offer insights into potential pressures or influences.

Warning Signs and How to Get Help

If you suspect your teen is drinking excessively, signs to look out for include frequent mood swings, neglecting responsibilities, secretive behavior, and changes in social circles. If these signs are evident, seeking professional help, counseling, or support groups might be necessary.

Tobacco/Nicotine Products

Tobacco and nicotine, primarily consumed as cigarettes, e-cigarettes, and Zyns (smokeless nicotine pouches that are placed under the top lip), can be alluring to teens, especially as e-cigarettes and Zyns have been developed with many attractive sounding flavors for young people. There certainly has been a glamorization of smoking in the past, making it seem like a rite of passage or a symbol of rebellion. Nowadays, smokeless alternatives are popular among teens. Despite repeated denials, the companies making these products are actively marketing them to our teens, particularly on social media and in feeds we will never see as adults. They contain the highly addictive substance nicotine, which can cause lung inflammation, throat and mouth irritation, headache, cough, and nausea. E-cigarettes often contain other flavorings which can cause lung disease. The bottom line about nicotine is that it can affect the developing brain, and we know from Chapter 2 how much work there is still to do in that area in teenagers.

Why Teens Use These Products

The reasons for starting can vary. For some, it's the allure of doing something "adult" or "forbidden." For others, it's peer pressure or the misconception that smoking is a stress reliever. The addictive nature of nicotine, a primary component of tobacco, ensures that what might start as experimental use can quickly become a habit.

Warning Signs

Changes in fragrance (smelling like smoke), frequent use of breath mints or gum, yellowing of teeth, and respiratory issues can be signs of tobacco use. If you identify these signs, consider counseling or support groups to help your teen quit. E-cigarettes/vapes produce vapor, but it will be even harder to detect the use of smokeless alternatives like Zyns. It's like the secret delivery of an addictive substance, nicotine, which can ultimately lead to life-long addiction if it continues for a length of time. The signs of nicotine dependency can be detected within a few days or weeks of occasional use, well before nicotine is used on a daily basis.

Consequences and Health Effects

The adverse effects of tobacco/nicotine are well-documented. Short-term effects include respiratory issues, decreased stamina, and reduced ability to taste and smell. In the long run, smoking can lead to heart disease, stroke, and various cancers, primarily lung. Additionally, tobacco use can lead to yellowed teeth, premature aging of the skin, and a persistent cough.

Talking with Your Teen About Tobacco/Nicotine

Discuss the myths and realities associated with smoking. Highlight the immediate and long-term effects. Most importantly, it debunks the notion that smoking is "cool" or beneficial in any way.

Prevention

- Education: Share statistics and real-life stories about the dangers of smoking.
- Stay Involved: Attend school or community-based prevention programs with your teen.
- Discuss Peer Pressure: Equip your teen with strategies to say "no."

In both the cases of alcohol and tobacco/nicotine, early intervention, open communication, and consistent support can go a long way in guiding our teens toward making informed and responsible choices.

Risk-Taking

The number of times I have willed that magic number of 25 when my teens' brain would be well on the way to being fully developed and their risk-taking behavior might have turned down a notch, and that's only with my firstborn. We must face the fact that we are in a time when risks seem exciting, and consequences feel like a distant mirage. While some risk-taking can be a healthy part of development, other risks have the potential for severe consequences. As a parent, you might wonder why risk-taking behavior seems so appealing to teenagers. Understanding the psychology behind this can help us better guide our children. You can turn back to Chapter 2 for even more clarification.

Why Do Teens Take Risks?

Contrary to popular belief, teenagers aren't just being defiant or rebellious when they take risks. Their brains are still developing, including the regions responsible for impulse control and judgment. This makes them more inclined to seek immediate rewards and less capable of assessing the potential consequences.

Common Risk-Taking Behaviors

Some common risky behaviors include unprotected sex, dangerous driving, substance abuse, and even illegal activities like shoplifting. Knowing what to look out for can help us stay one step ahead.

Encouraging Safe Risk-Taking

Not all risks are bad. You may have a teen who craves risk and risky activities. Safer risks, like trying go-karting or joining a mountain biking or rock climbing club, can benefit your teen's development. These activities provide the thrill of uncertainty and the reward of accomplishment but within a safe and controlled environment.

How to Keep Risk-Taking Teens Safe

- Open Communication: Talk openly about the types of risks and their potential consequences.

Even showing your teen pictures of potential outcomes can be helpful.
- Set Boundaries: Make it clear what behaviors are unacceptable and stick to those boundaries.
- Be a Role Model: Display healthy risk-taking in your life.

Support for Handling Risky Behavior

Sometimes, despite our best efforts, our teens engage in risky behavior. Professional counseling, peer support groups, and family therapy can be invaluable resources when this happens.

I am not inclined to lay down any magic formula here regarding punishments and consequences. The most important 'rules' about consequences and setting them are:

1. Don't make them in the moment; hear your child out and return to them with a consequence once you've cooled off (it could even be 24 hours). You can even, and my husband and I have done this, discuss with them the most appropriate consequence.

2. Please don't give a consequence that you have no chance of carrying out; it will dilute the process and leave you vulnerable.

Unprotected Sex

Unprotected sex is an alarming risk because of the immediate and possible long-term repercussions it can have. From unwanted pregnancies to sexually transmitted infections, the stakes are high. This isn't just a matter of physical health; it's about emotional wellbeing, too. If you can have an open and honest conversation about even embarking on sex, that would be a first step, and then discussing the importance of protection is crucial. And this isn't a one-time talk; it's an ongoing dialogue. The more you can make space for open communication before we get to this stage, the better.

I have always tried to have a very open and honest relationship with my children when they ask about sex. Answer honestly and age-appropriately. The same goes for risk-taking sexual behavior. Try not to judge but be open-minded and talk to them in the context of their generation.

Dangerous Driving

According to the American Academy of Child and Adolescent Psychiatry, car accidents are the leading cause of death in teens. Several factors contribute to this statistic, such as a lack of experience and a higher likelihood of taking risks like speeding or texting while driving.

This was my son's (inevitable) 4th risk-taking activity after dangerous surfing and skateboarding and then marijuana. Remember the night-time joy ride that kicked off this book?

Well, it got a whole lot worse. Canyons. Speed while driving the canyons above Los Angeles's Pacific Coast Highway. We dealt with this by giving our son a means of driving fast in a safer environment and taking him regularly to an excellent high-level go-karting track. If you have one, the risk-takers may switch one for another, so beware. It's like a fundamental need to be met in some of these teens- try to introduce them to something that will meet that need but in a more controlled environment. We weren't spared the crashes (that would be 2), but they were more minor, and he's alive.

How to Promote Safe Driving

- Education: Ensure your teen completes a comprehensive driver's education program.
- Practice: Spend plenty of time practicing driving in various conditions.
- Set Rules: Clearly define what is and is not acceptable when they are behind the wheel.
- Ensure your teen knows the laws around teen driving from their DVLA handbook.

Warning Signs and What to Do

It may be a red flag if you notice a change in your teen's driving behavior, like speeding tickets. In such cases, revisit the rules and consider additional driver's education or even postponing unsupervised driving.

By understanding why teens naturally take risks, we can create strategies to guide them toward making safer choices. It's not about stifling their sense of adventure but channeling it into activities that offer growth without endangering their wellbeing. As parents, we can't eliminate risk from our children's lives, but we can equip them with the tools to navigate those risks wisely.

Illegal Activities

When a teenager engages in illegal activities, the stakes are high. We're not just talking about the immediate risks of getting caught but also the long-term consequences, including legal repercussions and a tarnished record. These activities can range from shoplifting and vandalism to more severe offenses like drug dealing or even violent crimes.

Why Teens Engage in Illegal Activities

Sometimes, the allure of illegal activities is an extension of the thrill-seeking behavior that comes with the teenage years. The desire for quick rewards and an underdeveloped sense of consequence can make illegal activities seem enticing. Peer pressure can also be a significant factor, as can the desire for a reputation that comes with "living on the edge."

Consequences and Ramifications

Engaging in illegal activities isn't just about breaking the law; it has a ripple effect that extends far beyond the immediate moment. Legal repercussions can range from fines and community service to more severe penalties like imprisonment. The social and emotional fallout can be equally devastating, affecting friendships, family dynamics, and future employment opportunities.

Talking About Illegal Activities

It's crucial to create a space where open dialogue about the risks and consequences of illegal activities can occur. Often, the fear of punitive measures from parents can make teens less likely to share or seek guidance. This isn't a conversation to be tackled aggressively but needs a calm and rational approach. It may take some time for a teen to open up or admit to certain activities that they may be embarrassed or feel guilty about. Give them opportunities to open up. Put your phone down, look them in the eye, and show you have time for them. It may not happen the first, 3rd, or 10th time, but be patient. They just might in the end, and it may save them from going down a more dangerous path or may just improve your relationship.

Preventative Measures

- Education: Information is power. Make sure your teen knows the potential legal repercussions of illegal activities.
- Peer Influence: Know who your teen hangs out with and encourage friendships that are a positive influence.
- Be Engaged: Show interest in your teen's life and activities.

Fighting

Physical fights among teenagers are unfortunately all too common and can escalate quickly, leading to severe injuries or even criminal charges. While some teens describe fighting as a way to earn respect or defend themselves, the risks are never worth the perceived benefits.

One of my son's 9th-grade antics involved setting up an illicit fight club, which I mentioned before. Yes, these were a few turbulent, rocky years!

Why Teens Resort to Fighting

Physical aggression can sometimes be an outlet for emotional stress, frustrations, or insecurities. The teenage years can be full of turbulent emotions and social pressures, which can sometimes manifest as physical altercations. Hormonal changes can also contribute to heightened emotions and decreased impulse control. Although the school banned it and issued consequences (suspension) within a day, I was amazed at the number of students who wanted in on this, to fight, not just to watch. He was an organizer, but there was clearly a need for an outlet for pent-up emotions and feelings. If that were my child, we'd be off to the boxing gym or wrestling team!

Consequences and Ramifications

Physical fights can lead to immediate harm, such as injuries, but the consequences don't stop there. There can be legal repercussions, suspension from school, or even expulsion. Beyond the immediate consequences, fighting can result in long-lasting emotional trauma or ongoing conflicts.

Talking About Fighting

Initiating a conversation about fighting can be challenging but is necessary. Discuss the dangers involved and better ways to handle conflict. Stress the importance of your teen walking away and seeking adult intervention when faced with a potentially violent situation.

Strategies to Prevent Fighting

- Conflict Resolution Skills: Teach your teen how to resolve conflicts peacefully.

- Emotional Intelligence: Help them understand and manage their emotions.
- Safe Spaces: Ensure they know where to go or who to turn to when they feel threatened.

By understanding the factors that contribute to risky behavior like illegal activities and fighting, we can better prepare ourselves to guide our teenagers through issues like these. Providing them with the information they need, setting clear boundaries, and maintaining open lines of communication can go a long way in helping them make better choices. This also includes knowing when professional intervention is required. It may be a bumpy road, but we can help our teens navigate it safely with the right tools.

Truancy

One of the concerns that can often go overlooked in the mix of riskier behaviors, like drug use or fighting, is truancy. However, skipping school shouldn't be dismissed as a simple act of teenage rebellion. It can be a warning sign of deeper issues affecting your teen, and the consequences can be far-reaching.

Why Teens Skip School

There's a myriad of reasons why teens might decide to skip school. Some may be struggling academically and find it easier to avoid school altogether. Others may face social issues, such as bullying, that make the school environment unbearable. Sometimes, it's a case of feeling disconnected from the school community, feeling that their educational experience is not relevant or valuable to their lives.

Consequences and Ramifications

Truancy doesn't just affect your teen's academic performance; it can have broader implications. Habitual absence from school can lead to academic failure and, in the long run, limit job prospects. It can also contribute to other risky behaviors, as unmonitored time can often lead to undesirable activities like substance abuse or petty crimes.

Talking About Truancy

The key to addressing truancy is understanding the root cause. Dialogue should be initiated delicately, allowing your teen to express their concerns or reasons for skipping school without fear of immediate punishment.

Strategies to Address Truancy

- Consult School Officials: Meet with teachers or counselors to discuss any academic or social issues your teen might face.
- Set a Routine: A consistent routine can often make it easier for teens to attend school regularly.

- Seek Professional Help: If the truancy is a symptom of deeper emotional or psychological issues, consider seeking the help of a therapist or counselor.

Raising a teenager comes with its own set of challenges and rewards. One of the most daunting aspects can be navigating the various risks teens are prone to. This chapter delved into some of the riskier behaviors that teenagers are known for, ranging from substance abuse to truancy. We explored some of the reasons behind these behaviors and the potential consequences, providing a comprehensive guide on effectively addressing these issues. Armed with knowledge and proactive strategies, you CAN make a difference. By maintaining open communication and setting clear but flexible boundaries, you can guide your teen toward making better choices that will benefit them in the long run.

Chapter Takeaways

Substance Use

1. Know the Substances: Awareness of commonly abused substances like drugs, alcohol, and tobacco/nicotine is essential, and be aware of the warning signs that this may be becoming a problem.
2. Identify the Why: Understanding why teens are attracted to these substances can help formulate preventive strategies.

3. Consequences are Real: Make sure both you and your teen understand the short-term and long-term consequences of substance use.
4. Open Dialogue: Regular, non-judgmental communication about these topics is crucial. Consequences need to be reasonable, and you need to commit to them.

Risk-Taking Behaviors

1. Understand the Psychology: The teenage brain is wired for risk-taking, often without fully understanding the consequences.
2. Channel it Properly: Not all risks are harmful. Encourage safe risk-taking to allow room for growth and learning.
3. Boundaries Matter: Set clear expectations and boundaries to guide behaviors.

Specific Risky Behaviors

1. Unprotected Sex: Ongoing dialogue about protection is crucial.
2. Dangerous Driving: Make sure your teen is well-educated and well-practiced in driving safety and knows the laws around driving as a minor,

particularly who they are allowed to have in the car.

3. Illegal Activities: Understand and address the allure openly and calmly.
4. Fighting: Teach conflict resolution skills and emotional intelligence to deal with aggression.
5. Truancy: Address underlying issues that make your teen want to skip school.

General Strategies

1. Be Present: Your involvement in your teen's life cannot be overstated.
2. Be a Role Model: Teens are more likely to emulate the behaviors they see in you.
3. Professional Help: Know when it's time to seek external assistance, whether it's counseling or medical intervention.
4. Always go back to Chapter 1 and the seven steps; trust and maintain connection and always keep the lines of communication open.

CHAPTER 7
All About Friendships, Relationships, and Sex

In the teenage years, our children begin to take the crucial steps towards shaping their social circles, forming deep connections, and even venturing into the world of romantic relationships and sexual exploration. This journey can be filled with joy, wonder, curiosity, a fair amount of uncertainty, and even anxiety. As parents, we are responsible for (figuratively) walking alongside them, providing guidance and support as they navigate this new and complex landscape, if and when they need it or reaching out for it. Remember, we didn't embark on this with the addition of social media and all that it brings to friendships and relationships.

Arming ourselves with knowledge and a compassionate understanding of these subjects is critical to guiding our teens toward cultivating healthy relationships and navigating their sexuality responsibly. By equipping ourselves with this understanding, we can become the trusted advisors our teens need during these formative years.

Remember, as a parent, your role isn't just to set boundaries; it's also to help your teen understand the why behind them, encourage positive behaviors, and navigate the emotional intricacies these years bring with them. As we explore the details, I hope this chapter will provide the guidance you need to support your teenager on their journey confidently.

Friendships

As I've experienced with my children, teenage years are marked by transitions and transformations, and friendships play a vital role in navigating these changes. Friendships are more than just having someone to chat with or share activities with. They shape our teens' perceptions of their social world, influence their behavior, and significantly impact their mental health. Understanding the intricate dynamics of teen friendships and the effects of peer pressure can help us guide our teens through this critical stage of their lives.

Let's first look at the importance of quality over quantity in teenage friendships. It's not the number of friends that matters; it's the quality of these friendships. Teenagers, like adults, need close, supportive, and reliable friendships. These types of friendships provide a sense of belonging, boost self-esteem, and give them the emotional support they need. As parents, we can encourage our teens to seek quality friendships by discussing what makes a good friend and the value of deep, meaningful connections over casual acquaintances. My daughter Nina, who has quite an extraordinarily high emotional intelligence for her age, craved friends she could have deep and meaningful conversations with. She didn't need a lot of friends and enjoyed her alone time, but she wanted the friends she had to open up with and share and discuss the intricacies of their emotional lives. It took her a while to find what she was looking for; some would find it intense, but after middle school and pandemic social difficulties, she is much happier with her friends now and has learned how to handle and respect these friendships better.

You can ensure your teens know what a 'good quality' friend is. Good friends respect each other's individuality. They are honest, trustworthy, supportive, and encouraging. Good friends don't pressure each other into uncomfortable situations but respect boundaries and personal choices. They stand by each other in times of trouble and celebrate each other's successes. I've always had a strong sense of my commitment to good friends. Sometimes friends disappoint, but that can sometimes be us expecting too much. I've always talked with Nina about friend expectations and troubles of my own, and it's helped her. Even the idea that adults go through the same trials and tribulations with their friends can be helpful; it's a journey whenever you decide someone is your friend.

Encourage your teens to reflect on their friendships in light of these qualities. Are their friends supportive and respectful? Do they feel valued and accepted?

Have your teen regularly reflect on who in their friendship circle positively influences them. Picture a small circle and another one a little larger around it, then another. Perhaps their close family-parents and siblings will be dots on that inner circle, and then other friendships and family members in outer circles, depending on how positive/close they are. Make sure they know to move someone to an outer circle if that relationship is changing in a less healthy way. It's a helpful exercise to play throughout life, for you and your teen, and always to know who is in your inner circle.

We've had our fair share of friendship issues and social struggles. For our son, even one or two close friends were enough in the end after years of social struggles. I've already mentioned Nina's craving for emotional connection with her friends.

While peer pressure is often portrayed negatively, it's essential to understand it can also be positive. It can encourage healthy behaviors, like studying hard, participating in sports, or engaging in volunteer activities. However, negative peer pressure, leading to risky behaviors like substance abuse, reckless driving, or underage drinking, is a significant concern.

It's essential to have open conversations with our teens about peer pressure. Discuss scenarios they may encounter and brainstorm responses. For example, if they're offered a vape or an alcoholic drink, what could they say? Role-play can be beneficial, allowing them to practice saying no in a safe environment.

Social media plays a significant role in teen friendships and can amplify peer pressure. With constant access to their peers' activities and opinions, teens can feel immense pressure to fit in, often resulting in anxiety and low self-esteem. As parents, we can guide our teens to use social media responsibly, encouraging them to take regular breaks and reminding them that online life is often a highlight reel, not an accurate representation of reality. Please encourage them to take social media off their phone, even for a trial period-you could even do the same. It might have quite an impact that they had not expected.

Supporting your teen in their friendships is a delicate balance. It's not about controlling who they befriend but equipping them with the skills to make wise decisions. These six steps could be valuable:

1. Discuss the value of honesty in friendships. Honesty builds trust, and trust is the foundation of any strong relationship.

2. Point out good qualities in their peers, encouraging them to seek friends with similar attributes.

3. Help them bond over shared interests. Encourage your teen to join clubs or activities to meet like-minded peers.

4. Respect your teen's socializing style. Some teens prefer one-on-one interactions, while others thrive in group settings. My son still finds groups hard and is much more comfortable one-on-one. My teenage daughter is very happy at a party with many friends and one-on-one interactions. There is never one size fits all; they are unique and wonderfully individual! Respect them, and don't worry about their need to be alone, too; socializing is exhausting.

5. Model healthy friendships in your own life. Show them what mutual respect, trust, and positive communication look like.
6. Encourage your teen to trust their judgment. If a friendship feels draining or toxic, it's okay to step back. (Remember the circles.)

Nurturing healthy friendships is an ongoing process. There will be moments of joy and disappointment, but these experiences will help your teen learn and grow. And most importantly, let them know that as they navigate this territory, you're there for them every step of the way.

Open dialogue is critical in guiding our teens through these complexities. By keeping communication lines open, we can support our teens in fostering positive, enriching friendships and navigating peer pressure effectively.

Teen Relationships, Sexuality, and Consent

As parents, it's natural for us to feel a little apprehensive when our teenagers start to explore romantic relationships and their sexuality. These are delicate topics, filled with complex emotions, potential risks, and significant learning opportunities. We must create a space where they feel comfortable discussing their feelings, concerns, and queries. In this section, we'll explore how to handle these conversations with your teen, focusing on healthy relationships, safe sex practices, and the critical concept of consent.

Teenagers are at an age where romantic feelings and sexual curiosity start to surface, and these feelings can be confusing. It's crucial for us, as parents, to provide them with accurate information and guidance. We must remember to speak with our teenagers about relationships and sex in a positive, healthy light rather than focusing only on the potential risks and dangers. Emphasizing the importance of mutual respect, trust, and communication within a relationship is as important as discussing the possible consequences of risky sexual behaviors. This is a crucial time when teenagers are exploring their sexual identity and may or may not need a listening ear. Indeed, making ourselves available is vital.

Consent

The concept of consent is essential when discussing relationships and sex with your teenagers. Consent is a voluntary, mutual agreement to engage in specific activities without coercion or manipulation. It is a cornerstone of every respectful, healthy relationship, and your teenager must understand this. Talk about the different aspects of consent with your teenager - it must be explicit, it can be withdrawn at any time, and silence or the absence of 'no' doesn't mean 'yes.'

I like the cup of tea analogy, of course, being English. If you ask someone if they want a cup of tea, and they say 'yes, please,' then that's very clear. If they say 'no thank you,' that's also very clear. If they say yes and then by the time you've boiled the kettle and made the tea, they say no, then it's a no; you wouldn't force someone to drink tea if they said no. They may say yes to tea on a Saturday but not the following Thursday. That's also clear. It's also safe to say that someone might be awake and want tea, but by the time you get it to them, they are asleep or even unconscious, and you wouldn't then pour tea down their throat. Teaching or reminding your teen of this analogy to demonstrate consent is easy to grasp.

Engaging your teenager in scenario-based conversations can help them understand how to practice and respect consent. Ask them how they would handle certain situations, like if a partner changes their mind about sexual activity at the last minute or if a partner agrees to sex under the influence of alcohol or drugs. These conversations can prepare them for real-life situations and emphasize respecting others' boundaries.

It's also essential for teenagers to understand that everyone has different comfort levels when expressing love and affection. Reiterate that there's no rush when it comes to physical intimacy. They should never feel pressured into sexual activity - whether this pressure comes from a partner, friends, or societal expectations. Encourage them to listen to their feelings and respect their boundaries.

When discussing sex with older teens, it's crucial to address the importance of safe sex practices. Many of us will want our teens to wait as long as possible before embarking on this, for many different reasons, but education for the future is key. It's beneficial to understand the purpose of various contraceptive methods, how they operate, and their effectiveness in preventing sexually transmitted infections (STIs) and unplanned pregnancies.

Types of Contraceptive Methods and Their Effectiveness

- Condoms: Effective at preventing both STIs and unplanned pregnancies when used correctly.
- Birth Control Pills/Implants/Injections (hormonal methods): Highly effective against unplanned pregnancies but do not protect against STIs.
- Intrauterine Devices (IUDs): Highly effective at preventing pregnancies but do not offer STI protection.
- Emergency Contraception: Effective when used within a specific time frame after unprotected sex, but not a regular method for STI prevention or contraception.

Resources and Where to Access Them

To get more information and help, consider reaching out to the following resources:

1. Healthcare Providers: Consult your general physician or a specialized healthcare provider for personalized advice.

2. Sexual Health Clinics: Many cities have clinics dedicated to sexual health where you can get confidential consultations and access to contraceptives.
3. Websites and Online Platforms: Websites such as Planned Parenthood offer valuable information and even have online chat support.
4. Pharmacies: Over-the-counter contraceptives like condoms and some emergency contraceptive pills can be obtained without a prescription.
5. Educational Institutions: Some schools and colleges offer sexual health education and may provide access to free or low-cost contraceptives.

By seeking information and guidance from these resources, your teen can take responsibility and make more informed choices about their sexual health.

Remember that these conversations about relationships, sexuality, and consent should not be a one-time talk but rather an ongoing dialogue. Let your teenager know that they can approach you with any questions or concerns, whatever your views are personally. Reassure them that it's okay to make mistakes and that they can learn and grow from these experiences.

Chapter Takeaways

Friendships

1. Quality Over Quantity: Encourage your teen to focus on the quality of friendships rather than the number of friends. Good friendships offer emotional support and a sense of belonging and boost self-esteem.

2. Identifying Good Friends: Help your teen identify what makes a good friend, including traits like honesty, trustworthiness, and respect for boundaries.

3. Peer Pressure: Teach your teen that peer pressure can be both positive and negative. Equip them with strategies to handle negative peer pressure effectively.

4. Role of Social Media: Guide your teen to use social media responsibly. Emphasize that online life is often not an accurate representation of reality.

5. Six Points for Healthy Friendships: Discuss honesty, point out good qualities in peers, help them find common interests, respect their socializing style, model healthy friendships, and encourage them to trust their judgment.

Teen Relationships, Sexuality, and Consent

1. Open Dialogue: Encourage open and ongoing conversations about relationships and sexuality. Make sure your teen feels comfortable approaching you with questions or concerns.

2. Positive Framing: While discussing relationships and sex, focus not just on risks but also on the positive aspects like mutual respect, trust, and emotional connection.

3. Understanding Consent: Make sure your teen understands the concept of consent and its importance in any relationship.

4. Safe Sex Practices: Talk openly about contraception methods and their effectiveness. Encourage your teen to make informed decisions about sexual health.

5. No Rush for Intimacy: Teach your teen that there's no rush to engage in sexual activities and that respecting personal boundaries is crucial.

6. Resources: Provide resources such as healthcare providers, sexual health clinics, and online platforms where they can get more information and support.

CHAPTER 8

Supporting Your Teen's Education and Empowering Them for the Future

As a mother, I am very much aware of the challenges that teenagers face when navigating their academics and transitioning into adulthood. It's a complex world filled with pressures, changes, and expectations. This chapter will give you the tools to guide, support, and empower your teen through these transformative years, incorporating the 7-step framework for effective parenting.

Our children's educational success significantly shapes their future. However, achieving this success isn't only about keeping up with their homework or getting the highest grades—it's about encouraging a balanced perspective on academic pressure and college choices. We must foster an environment that allows our teens to strive for excellence, but not at the expense of their mental health and wellbeing. Of course, we all enter into this with preconceived expectations. The more open-minded you can be with your teen, the more you can focus on your family and your child's needs, and the more you can avoid comparing with other families, the better!

And let's not forget, we're not just raising students; we're raising future adults. Our job doesn't stop at the school gate. It is equally important to foster responsibility and independence, preparing them for life beyond the classroom. By doing so, we equip them with the confidence and skills to take control of their lives and make informed decisions about their future.

Essential life skills such as financial literacy and money management are not often taught in school, but they play a pivotal role in our teens' journey into adulthood. Empowering them with these skills not only secures their financial future but also instills a sense of responsibility and self-reliance.

Leadership and community involvement are vital for their personal development. They help our teens understand the value of teamwork, empathy, and civic responsibility. By encouraging their participation in community activities, we are helping them to become well-rounded individuals ready to make positive contributions to society.

Finally, we must help our children build resilience and develop coping skills. Life won't always be smooth sailing. They'll face trials and hardships along the way. It's not about shielding them from these challenges but equipping them with the tools they need to work through them.

In this chapter, we will delve into these topics, providing you with practical guidance and actionable steps to support your teen's education and empower them for the future. Remember, our goal is to nurture a deep bond with our teens, all while helping them thrive and excel in life.

Academic Pressure and College Choices: Encouraging a Balanced Perspective

As a parent and medical professional, I've seen the effects of academic pressure on teenagers. I've witnessed it in my children and numerous young patients I've treated over the years. It's a real struggle that affects both the mental and physical health of our teens.

The desire to excel academically is not inherently harmful. We naturally want the best for our children, and education is a crucial pillar for their future success. But we must be mindful about the amount of pressure we put on them. I remember when my eldest son was applying to colleges, I knew he needed to decide where he felt comfortable. My husband and I took a blinkered approach and decided to filter out all the noise around grades, colleges, SATs, and APs we were hearing and seeing on the school's social media pages and from fellow parents. We knew our son, always marching to the beat of his own drum, needed to forge his own path, and we couldn't just impose our ideas and expectations on him.

For a start, he wouldn't excel that way and wouldn't own this next chapter of his life, setting him up for possible failure. As it turned out, he found the perfect solution for him, and he combined studying at a US college in Madrid (Saint Louis

University) with playing soccer in the Madrid league. We would never have found this for him. It took him time to generate the motivation to find his path, which was slightly nerve-wracking, but ultimately, he found a great solution.

Navigating college choices is a significant part of this journey. It can be stressful for teens as they feel they are making decisions that will impact their entire future. And there is so much choice it can be pretty overwhelming. It's crucial to let them know that they have options. Not everyone is meant for Ivy League schools or even traditional four-year colleges, and they may also be prohibitively expensive. It's also very reasonable to point out that yes, research shows that a college degree ultimately can lead to higher earnings and more career success, but you're not continually asked where you went to school -that is less consequential in the end, even though it might seem like the be all and end all at the time. Help them gain some perspective on this to take the pressure off.

An essential part of our role as parents is to encourage a balanced perspective. We need our teens to understand that while academic success is important, it doesn't define their value or future success. It's about helping them see that their self-worth is not tied to their grades or the college they get into. Their value lies in their character, kindness, ability to overcome adversity, and passion for their interests.

When dealing with academic pressure, taking several steps to maintain open communication with your teen is essential.

Step 1: Initiate the Conversation

Start by asking your teen how they feel about their future beyond high school. This opens the door for them to share their emotions and plans with you.

Step 2: Active Listening

Pay close attention to their worries, hopes, and dreams. Your role here is not to offer immediate solutions but to listen empathetically.

Step 3: Offer Reassurance

Let them know it's perfectly okay to ask for help when feeling overwhelmed. Reassure them that everyone faces challenges and that they're not alone.

Step 4: Encourage Stress Management Techniques

Finally, please encourage them to explore stress management techniques such as mindfulness (discussed in Chapter 3), yoga, or journaling. These can be valuable tools for coping with academic stress.

Remember that every child is different, and so is their path to success. As parents, our role is to guide and support them without imposing our dreams and expectations on them. It's about helping them find their path and applauding them every step of the way, regardless of where it leads. They will be aware of our path, and it will be in their mind, even if we don't actively discuss it.

Ensure they understand that while academics are important, they're not the be-all and end-all. Above all, let's remind them that they are more than their grades or the college they attend. They are unique individuals with diverse talents and capabilities, all worth celebrating. You may even need to discuss this with your child's school if you find their expectations are different from your child's. They have a different agenda again, wanting their students to attend specific colleges. YOU, as the parents, are the only ones who can have solely your child in your sites and can help steer them towards a future, college or not, that is right for them.

Ensure that your teen takes advantage of all the resources available at school, including their advisor, college counseling, seminars about college entrance, college fairs, and other online and in-person activities surrounding this. Many colleges have online tours nowadays to make drawing up lists easier.

Our ultimate goal is to see our children grow into well-rounded, confident, happy adults ready to take on the world in their own unique way.

Fostering Responsibility and Independence: Preparing Teens for Adulthood

I've found that one of the most rewarding aspects of being a parent is witnessing your child's transformation from a dependent youngster to an independent and responsible young adult, however challenging that might be along the way!

Some religions mark this transition with a ceremony or party. Our family devised the 13 challenges, a series of tasks and challenges that would need greater maturity and a sense of independence and empathy to carry out and complete. We then celebrated the completion of these tasks. Look out for my book "13 Challenges: Preparing Your Teen for the Future" coming soon.

It is hard to find that balance between protecting them and letting them learn from their experiences as they grow. There is a point where you have to transition to treating them more like an adult.

Fostering responsibility and independence in their teen years can be a delicate task. It involves gradually giving them more freedom and responsibility while still providing guidance and support. It's a bit like teaching a child to ride a bike—you need to hold on at first, but eventually, you need to let go and trust they won't fall. Think of it like a launch-you want to make sure the launch is successful, not a 'failed launch'. I heard that phrase from a friend telling me about her son, who agonized about a college place he had been given but ultimately did not, or could not, leave town.

We can start by providing them with age-appropriate responsibilities, such as household chores or part-time jobs. Setting clear expectations and letting them experience the consequences of not meeting them is crucial.

Here is a list of basic tasks that your teen should be successful at, or on the way to being successful at, by the time they leave for college:

- learning to drive and getting a driver's license, and starting to drive places on their own or helping with rides for younger siblings where appropriate,
- taking public transport
- doing their own laundry for at least a year before going away, but ideally from 16, if not before.
- cooking dinner for themselves (and the family if possible) regularly (try for once a month initially), and doing grocery shopping for the household regularly.
- making their breakfast and lunch at least a few times a week.
- running their own errands
- booking doctor and self-care appointments themselves
- managing the taking of any of their medications
- set up and use a calendar on their phone so that they take responsibility for appointments and activities
- taking over management of screen time and bedtime
- managing a weekly allowance for their spending and managing a debit card, online banking, and digital payment platforms.

Encourage them to make their own decisions and allow them to experience the results, whether good or bad. When Ted had to decide which classes to take in his senior year of high school, we discussed the pros and cons of his options, but ultimately, the final decision was his. This experience taught him the importance of informed decision-making and made him feel more in control of his life.

At the same time, it's crucial to maintain open communication with your teen. Reassure them that you're always there to support and guide them, even as they become more independent. After all, it's not about pushing them out of the nest, but ensuring they're ready to fly when they do leave.

Independence and responsibility are two critical skills your teen will need in adulthood. It might seem scary at first, both for you and them, but remember that it's all part of their growth. Through these experiences, they learn vital life skills, gain confidence in their abilities, and become prepared for the world beyond high school.

In the end, it's all about trust. Trust in your teen's abilities, trust in the values you've instilled in them, and trust in the process. It can be challenging, and there will undoubtedly be a few bumps along the way. But when you see your child standing on their own two feet, making responsible decisions, and confidently navigating the world, you'll know that all the challenges were worth it.

So let's continue guiding our teens, giving them the tools they need to be successful, and trusting them to make the right choices. After all, our job as parents is not to prepare the path for our children but to prepare our children for the path.

Essential Life Skills-Financial Literacy and Money Management: Paving the Path to Financial Independence

My traditional upbringing in England did not come with any money management tools, far from it. It was almost a taboo subject. I was pretty terrible at it for quite a while. Even now, I can improve at budgeting and planning our finances. Of course, money doesn't come with instructions; we certainly can—and should—teach our children how to handle it responsibly as best we can. And if you don't think you're the right person to do that, find a course on financial literacy geared to teens. I wish I had had that growing up.

In the context of my own family, it was the summer after my son turned 15 that I realized the significance of financial literacy. He was passionate about cars and go-karting and wanted to own a car. An advert came on the TV, and he said something to the effect of, I want that car!

I remember chuckling at his enthusiasm and recognizing the opportunity for a teachable moment. "Well, Ted," I said, "cars are expensive, not just to buy, but to run. Insurance, gas, maintenance—it all adds up, especially for a teen who is, understandably, a greater risk behind the wheel. Do you know how you're going to afford it?" He shrugged, his excitement dampened by the reality check.

Teaching your teen financial literacy and money management is about more than just preparing them to handle money. It's about helping them understand the value of money and its role in achieving their dreams and goals.

So, how can we equip our teens with these essential life skills?

Let's start with the basics. Open a savings account for your teen and teach them about saving and investing. Encourage them to set aside a portion of any money they receive—from their allowance, part-time jobs, or gifts—into their savings. Show them how compound interest works and the benefits of saving and investing early.

Take it a step further by introducing them to budgeting. I remember sitting down with Ted a few weeks after our talk to help him create his first budget. We wrote down all his income and expenses, and he quickly realized that the fancy sports car he wanted was well out of his reach—at least for now. It was a sobering moment for him, but it also motivated him to start saving, thinking more carefully about his spending, and ultimately sparking an entrepreneurial streak.

Then comes the concept of credit. It might seem too early, but with college on the horizon for many teens, understanding credit is crucial. Explain how credit cards work, the dangers of debt, and the importance of a good credit score. When Ted went to college, we got him a credit card with a small limit to help him build his credit history and learn to manage credit responsibly.

Financial literacy and money management are vital life skills that will serve your teen well into adulthood. And the sooner they learn these skills, the more time they have to practice and become comfortable managing their finances.

It's not a lesson that can be taught overnight. And even if you think you need to improve at it and are not some financial whizz or have a finance-related job, whatever you can teach them, even the basics, will be better than nothing. Trust me, as your child starts making smarter financial decisions and you see them taking control of their financial future, you'll know it was worth it.

Ultimately, it's not about how much money they have but what they do with it. As parents, let's equip our teens with the knowledge and skills they need to make intelligent financial decisions and set them up for a lifetime of financial success.

Encouraging Leadership and Community Involvement: Nurturing the Next Generation of Leaders and Active Citizens

The need for leadership skills and community involvement cannot be underestimated, especially for teens on the cusp of adulthood.

You may have a teen, like my son, who isn't super social, and the idea of joining the student council or some other similar organization seems horrifying. Well, many schools have community involvement and volunteering requirements, so he worked alongside me, cooking at a homeless shelter on numerous occasions. Again, modeling that behavior sends a powerful, strong message. I have also always been involved in advocacy work at our school district, and this certainly pays off in terms of setting that example of working for the greater good of the community and inspiring them to make a difference, if your work schedule allows.

You might wonder why these two facets—leadership and community involvement—are being discussed together. It's because they're two sides of the same coin. Leadership requires empathy, understanding, and a willingness to serve—all attributes fostered through active community involvement. The more we as parents can be involved with school and community activities, the more this will rub off and inspire our teens to follow us into this important work, maybe not now, but in the future.

Encourage your teen to step up in their everyday environments, whether in small or big ways. This could be at school, in a club, or even within their group of friends. Of course, every child is unique, and it's crucial to provide them with the opportunity that suits them best. It won't be the same for all your children; mine could not be more different and, with that, have differing needs.

One afternoon, my daughter came home excited about running for student council president. I saw the spark in her eyes—the raw ambition. But I knew she would face challenges. Instead of telling her how to lead, I asked questions. "What would you like to change at your school?" "How will you rally your friends behind your cause?" "What will you do if you don't win?" These questions made her think critically and approach the role with a problem-solving mindset.

Community involvement is another way to foster leadership. When teens engage in their communities, they understand their actions can make a difference. It promotes empathy and highlights the importance of collective effort. Encourage your teen to volunteer locally or join groups that aim to solve community issues.

My daughters and I have worked serving meals in Skid Row, Los Angeles. This is a raw, firsthand experience of many people's struggles not so far away from where we live. It has sparked many conversations about what more we can do and the inequality and disparities in our greater area.

As a parent, I have spent countless hours advocating for all children in our school district on several issues. I have always involved my children in these campaigns, and they have spoken at school board meetings with me, particularly on the issues of improving school food and returning to school during the pandemic to minimize learning loss. This has taught them invaluable lessons.

Fostering leadership and community involvement in your teen means guiding them to become responsible, empathetic, and proactive individuals. It's about helping them see the impact they can have, not just within their immediate circles but in the broader community, and my girls, particularly, have been involved with this firsthand.

Leading and serving in a community are about more than personal development; they're about making the world better, one small step at a time. By fostering these values in our teens, we're not just raising responsible adults but nurturing the next generation of leaders and active citizens. Our world needs them now more than ever.

Resilience and Coping Skills: Equipping Your Teen for Life's Hurdles

As a parent, there's a story I often share from my teenage years—a story of failure, heartache, and, ultimately, resilience. I desperately wanted to get into medical school but struggled with math at a higher level (the UK's 'A' level), one of the requirements for UK medical school. I failed the class and did not get the grade I needed to enter. I was crushed - all my friends were going off to University, and I was held back. I worked solidly for the next three months to retake the exam and succeeded in raising my grade to a high level. I even stayed home over Christmas while the rest of my family tried skiing for the first time. That resilience and the inability to give up became vital skills to learn as I progressed through medical school and the slog of working as a junior doctor in the UK. Try to instill in your children the desire never to give up. Being vulnerable and able to share harrowing stories from your past is so valuable to them. It can be incredibly powerful for your children, and you might be surprised at how little you have shared from your earlier life. With failure or setbacks along the way, their response to that and the resilience they show will help them through life.

Resilience isn't about never falling down; it's about learning how to get back up, dust off, and keep moving forward. It's the ability to cope with life's challenges and bounce back from adversity. In today's world, filled with uncertainties and constant decision-making, resilience is a critical skill every teen needs.

I'm sure you're asking, "But how do I help my teen build resilience?" Well, let me share some strategies that worked for my children, and I hope they'll work for yours, too.

This seems counter-intuitive, but allowing your teen to experience failure is so important. Of course, our instinct is to protect our children from failure. But trust me, wrapping them in cotton wool does more harm than good. Life isn't a smooth ride. There will be bumps along the way, and it's through these challenging experiences that resilience is built.

When my son was cut from an elite club soccer team in a very abrupt way by a coach we all respected and trusted with his development, he was devastated. We could have stepped in, offered solutions, or tried to fix the situation. Instead, we allowed him to process his emotions and determine his next steps. He dusted himself off, tried out for another club, and has played high-level soccer ever since. It was painful to watch, but it was a pivotal moment in his journey to resilience.

Next, help your teen develop problem-solving skills. When faced with a problem, instead of jumping in to solve it for them, guide them through the process. Ask them open-ended questions that encourage them to think critically and develop solutions. This empowers them to face and overcome future challenges independently. I have definitely suffered from that role of wanting to be the 'fixer.' Resist! Know that, yes, sometimes you can fix things, BUT often, that is not the best path for the parent of a growing teen. Stop and think before you jump in with words or actions. You also need to accept that not everything can be fixed.

I remember when my daughter had a falling out with her best friend. She came to me, tears streaming down her face, asking for advice. I wanted to fix it, but I realized this was a chance for her to develop her problem-solving skills. So, instead of giving her the answers, we had a conversation. "What do you think you could do?" "How do you think she felt?" This dialogue encouraged her to empathize and think critically about resolving the conflict.

Lastly, model resilience. Our teens learn more from what we do than what we say. Show them that it's okay to make mistakes and face hardships. Let them see how you handle stress, overcome challenges, and bounce back from setbacks. You are their first and most impactful role model.

Resilience and coping skills are not attributes we're born with. They're cultivated over time through experience and guidance. As parents, we can't protect our teens from life's challenges, but we can equip them with the tools to face them with resilience. And remember, it's the process of getting back up after a fall that shapes us, not the fall itself. We are, after all, defined not by our challenges but by how we rise to meet them.

Chapter Takeaways

Academic Pressure and College Choices

1. Balanced Perspective: Encourage your teen to strive for academic excellence but not at the cost of their mental well-being.
2. Multiple Paths to Success: Openly discuss various educational pathways, such as vocational schools, community colleges, and gap years, not just top-tier universities.
3. Self-Worth Beyond Academics: Reinforce the idea that their value isn't solely tied to their academic achievements.
4. Steps for Open Communication: Start conversations, actively listen, offer reassurance, and introduce stress management techniques.

Fostering Responsibility and Independence

1. Age-Appropriate Responsibilities: Gradually give your teen more responsibilities, like chores or part-time jobs, to foster independence.
2. Decision-Making: Encourage your teen to make choices and bear the consequences, helping them develop crucial life skills.

3. The Art of Letting Go: Learn to trust your teen's judgment and abilities and give them the space to grow.

Essential Life Skills - Financial Literacy and Money Management

1. Start with Savings: Open a savings account for your teen and teach them the basics of saving and investing.

2. Budgeting Skills: Sit down with your teen to create their first budget, helping them understand income, expenses, and financial planning.

3. Credit Education: Teach your teen about credit cards, debt management, and the significance of a good credit score.

Encouraging Leadership and Community Involvement

1. Leadership Opportunities: Encourage your teen to take leadership roles in their community, school, or other social circles.

2. Community Engagement: Strongly suggest your teen actively participates in community services, fostering empathy and civic responsibility.

3. Critical Thinking: Instead of providing solutions, ask open-ended questions to stimulate their problem-solving abilities.

Resilience and Coping Skills

1. Allow Room for Failure: Let your teen experience setbacks and challenges, vital for building resilience.

2. Problem-Solving: When your teen faces a problem, guide them through the thinking process to find solutions rather than solve it for them.

3. Model Resilience: Demonstrate your resilience in facing challenges to inspire your teen.

CHAPTER 9

Building a Lasting Connection: The Parent-Teenager Relationship in Adulthood

"Life doesn't come with a manual; it comes with a mother." I saw this quote on a greeting card once, and it made me chuckle, but it also struck a chord with me. Indeed, mothers (and fathers) are the first guides in our lives, but parenting, especially during the teenage years, can often feel like assembling a complex puzzle without a reference picture. And just when you think you're getting the hang of it, your teenagers start maturing into young adults.

This transition may be daunting for both parents and teens. It's a time when the relationship dynamics shift, the roles evolve, and the parenting style you've adhered to over the years will need to be adjusted. But despite these challenges, it's also a phase of immense growth and an opportunity to strengthen the bond with your child.

Building and *maintaining a lasting connection* with your teen as they transition into adulthood is a continuous process that brings us full circle back to a reminder of the seven steps:

Shift from 'Top-Down' Parenting to Mentoring: As your child becomes a young adult, they need more of a mentor who can guide them and actively listen to their issues and concerns.

Nurture Emotional Intimacy: Make time for one-on-one conversations, activities, and bonding experiences that build trust and emotional closeness. Here, you will demonstrate the trust you've established by being genuine and honest in your interactions and showing that you value their thoughts and feelings.

Foster Open Communication and Dialogue: Encourage your teen to share their thoughts, feelings, and concerns openly with you and reciprocate by actively listening and providing constructive feedback where needed, making sure they feel their voice is being heard and that they are valued.

Respect Their Independence: Give them the space to make their own decisions and learn from their experiences while being there to support them when needed. Setting boundaries and respecting their space but also ensuring their safety.

Support Personal and Professional Goals: Be supportive of their ambitions, whether educational, career-oriented, or personal, and provide the resources and guidance they may need to achieve them. This is where bolstering self-esteem and encouragement plays a crucial role, ensuring they always have the confidence to chase their dreams.

By taking these steps, you can create a strong foundation for a lasting, meaningful relationship with your teen as they mature into adulthood. Throughout this journey, always practice emotional intelligence and be a positive role model. This will guide their interactions with others and shape their emotional growth.

Remember my firstborn, Ted? Since leaving home, he has traveled from Madrid to Poland, to Ghana, and now to the UK, and he continues to forge his unique path. He was once that rebellious teenager who tested every bit of my patience. I can now see that the tumultuous teenage years were not merely a phase of rebellion but a crucial time for him to carve out his identity and grow. As his parents, it was not only our job to guide him during these formative years but also to shift my role from a more 'top-down' parent to a mentor as he matured into an adult.

In this chapter, we will explore this transition, offering guidance on adapting to these changes while keeping the lines of communication open, supporting your child's ambitions, engaging in shared activities, and respecting their privacy. The goal is to build a bond that will not just withstand the challenges of adolescence but continue to flourish in adulthood.

■ Moving from Parenting to Mentoring

If you were to look at parenting as a spectrum, with 'top-down' parenting on one end and permissive parenting on the other, mentoring would sit comfortably in the middle, striking a balance. As your teenager begins to transition into adulthood, so should your parent role evolve into more of a mentorship role.

Ted, my oldest, and I were at loggerheads for the longest time. We argued over curfews, study schedules, and food preferences, which strained the relationship. But I realized that our rules were pushing him away instead of protecting him. My role needed to change from an enforcer to a mentor, fostering a more balanced relationship based on mutual respect and open dialogue.

But what does moving from parenting to mentoring entail?

Mentoring, unlike parenting, is less about enforcing rules and more about guiding your teenager toward making sound decisions. It involves providing them with the tools to handle life's challenges independently and fostering a relationship based on trust, open communication, and respect.

The first step towards transitioning from a parent to a mentor is acknowledging and respecting your teenager's emerging adulthood. It's about understanding that they are no longer children but budding adults capable of taking on responsibilities and making informed decisions.

I remember the day when Ted came home from school and announced that he had decided on his college major. Rather than questioning his decision or offering unsolicited advice, I asked him to tell me more about why he made that choice. That conversation marked a shift in our relationship. I was no longer directing his path; I was walking alongside him, offering guidance when needed.

As a mentor, respecting your teen's autonomy and giving them the space to make their own decisions, even if they make mistakes, is important. Remember, mistakes are not failures but learning opportunities. Encourage your teen to learn from their errors and grow rather than shielding them from the consequences.

Open communication is another critical aspect of mentoring. As a mentor, your goal should be to create a safe environment where your teen feels comfortable expressing their thoughts, concerns, and aspirations. To achieve this, you should be an active listener, giving your teen your undivided attention when they are speaking. This crucial step shows them that you value their opinions, which, in turn, encourages them to share more with you.

Keep in mind that mentoring doesn't mean you relinquish your parental responsibilities. It means adjusting them to accommodate your teenager's growing independence. It's about striking a balance between giving advice and letting your teen navigate their own path while providing a safety net of love, support, and guidance.

Lastly, remember to be patient. Transitioning from parenting to mentoring takes time. It is a gradual process that requires understanding and respect from both parties. It may be fraught with challenges, but it is a path worth treading as it paves the way for a more open, trusting, and mutually respectful relationship with your teen.

As Ted and I navigated this new relationship dynamic, I found that we were able to resolve our differences more amicably and grew closer as a result. Now, I see my son thriving, making responsible and exciting decisions, and learning from his mistakes. And that, to me, is a testament to the power of transitioning from parenting to mentoring.

Supporting Your Teen's Personal and Professional Goals

When it comes to their dreams and ambitions, being your teen's biggest cheerleader is crucial. We live in a world that's often quick to judge and slow to support, and our children need to know that home is a place where they can dream big and have the unwavering support they need to pursue those dreams. I've mentioned Ted's soccer several times; this has always been his passion. He's had knocks, injuries, and setbacks, but we kept going to those games, supporting him and his dreams.

My daughters have expressed their desire to pursue a career in the arts, specifically theater and musical theater. At first, my mind raced with concerns about the practicalities of such career choices. I worried about their financial stability, the competitiveness of those fields, and the challenges they might face. However, I realized that my role was not to critique or discourage them and their passion, but to support their dreams.

Understanding and supporting your teen's personal and professional goals involves several key elements. Firstly, listen and engage. It's essential to be open and receptive when your teen talks about their ambitions. Show genuine interest and ask questions that inspire them to think deeper about their aspirations. When Nina shared her artistic dreams with me, I encouraged her to talk more about her inspirations, what she hoped to express through her art, and where she envisioned it taking her.

Secondly, encourage exploration. It's normal for teenagers to be unsure about their future career paths, and our job as parents is to support them as they explore various fields of interest. Provide guidance, not direction. Remember, it's your teen's journey, not yours. While it's tempting to guide them towards what we believe is best for them, empowering them to make their own decisions is more important. We can provide resources, share our wisdom, and offer advice when asked, but the ultimate choice must be theirs.

Next, be prepared for change. Teenagers often change their minds as they grow and discover new interests, and that's perfectly okay. If they shift gears and explore a new path, be just as supportive, pivot like a pro, and be as you were with their previous ambition.

Then, offer emotional support. Pursuing personal and professional goals can be challenging, and there will inevitably be ups and downs. As a parent, your role is to offer a safe and supportive environment for your teen to express their frustrations and celebrate their victories. Let them know it's okay to fail, it's okay to feel unsure, and that every step they take, successful or not, is progress.

Finally, help them set and achieve realistic goals. This involves helping them break down their bigger dreams into smaller, more achievable steps and celebrating each milestone they reach along the way.

Supporting your teen's goals isn't just about nurturing their professional aspirations. It's about helping them discover their passions, build self-confidence, and cultivate the resilience they need to navigate the world. It may require patience, time, and resources, but nothing can compare to the joy of seeing your child pursue their dreams with tenacity and conviction.

Nurturing Emotional Intimacy and Open Communication

One of the most rewarding yet challenging aspects of raising a teenager is maintaining a strong emotional connection and facilitating open lines of communication. My son Ted is a brilliant but introspective young man and not especially social. Like many teenagers, he often found it challenging to express his emotions and thoughts freely.

Make sure to encourage open discussions, fostering an environment where your teenager feels safe to express themselves.

Practicing emotional honesty is another essential component. As parents, we feel the need to be the 'rock' for our children. But it's also vital to express our emotions and vulnerability, particularly as our children grow up and move towards adulthood. After all, we're human, too. It allowed Ted to see that having and expressing emotions is okay.

Respecting their privacy is equally essential. The teenage years are a time of exploration and self-discovery, and it's only natural that your teen will want to keep some thoughts and experiences to themselves. Make it clear that you respect their need for personal space and will not invade their privacy without cause.

Lastly, avoid criticism and judgment. If your teen feels judged, they're likely to close off communication. Instead, foster a supportive environment where they feel comfortable sharing their successes and failures. When Ted's grades slipped, I resisted the urge to criticize. Instead, I tried to approach the situation with understanding, asking, "How can we support you to help you improve?"

Nurturing emotional intimacy and open communication with your teen takes patience, understanding, and a lot of love. It's about creating a space where they feel understood, heard, and accepted. It's about proving to them, through your actions, that they can come to you with anything, no matter how big or small, without fear of judgment or criticism.

In our case, Ted is gradually opening up more, sharing his world with us. He understood that we were there to support him, not scold him and that we valued his thoughts, feelings, and experiences. And as he made his way, our bond grew stronger, thanks to our commitment to emotional intimacy and open communication.

Engaging in Shared Interests and Activities

Engaging in shared activities offers a unique opportunity to bond with your teen in a relaxed, organic setting. It's not about monitoring their every move or forcing them into activities that don't genuinely interest them. It's about finding common ground, a shared passion you can explore and enjoy together.

For Nina and me, a love of nature and outdoor activities brought us closer. Nina was naturally curious about the world, a spark that was hard to miss. She loved discussing and debating while going for neighborhood walks, especially during a beautiful sunset, or hiking in a nearby park if we had more time.

Our shared love of nature led us to a multitude of shared activities. Hiking became a staple in our weekly schedule. Not only did it provide us with a regular dose of much-needed physical activity, but it also offered an opportunity for meaningful conversations that may not have occurred within the four walls of our home. Something about the tranquility of the outdoors encouraged a deeper level of communication.

We also started baking bread together, which taught us patience and the importance of tending to relationships. It gave us a shared responsibility and a common goal. When we saw the fruits of our labor - the warm bloomer just out of the oven or the loaf made from our sourdough starter - it felt like a shared victory, something we had accomplished together.

During these times, Nina would open up about her dreams, fears, and hopes for the future. We talked, we laughed, and sometimes, we simply enjoyed the silence, knowing that the comforting presence of each other was enough.

It's important to remember that your teenager has their own set of interests, and it's your role as a parent to nurture those, even if they differ from yours. And when you find a shared interest, seize the opportunity to explore it together. It can pave the way for experiences and conversations that will bring you closer, helping to solidify your relationship during these critical years.

Our shared interests are a lifeline, a connection that will hold us together, even when teenage rebellion and hormonal changes threaten to drive us apart. It gives us something to talk about, to look forward to, and to experience together. Then, when Nina embarks on her life path, these shared experiences will continue to be a crucial component of our relationship, reminding us of the bond we share, no matter where life takes us.

Respecting Boundaries and Privacy in Adult Relationships

As parents, our instinct is to protect our children, to shield them from harm, and to help guide their decisions. But as our children evolve into young adults, we must learn to respect their boundaries and privacy. I confess that this was a challenging transition for me. It required understanding, patience, and, most importantly, trust.

One of the first things I had to come to terms with was respecting Ted's personal space. I remember when he first asked me to knock before entering his room. It caught me off guard, but it was a legitimate request. His room was his sanctuary, and he deserved the courtesy of privacy. It was a simple act, knocking before entering, but it symbolized our relationship's changing dynamics.

Equally important was understanding that Ted had a life outside of the home. He was building friendships, relationships, and experiences that were uniquely his. As much as I wanted to know every detail, I had to respect that some stories were his to tell in his own time. I had to learn to keep my nosiness in check!

This meant learning to listen without judgment, without the urge to offer advice immediately. There were times when he would share experiences or challenges he was facing, and I would have to hold my tongue, wait, and ask, "Do you want my advice, or do you just need someone to listen?" This is a hard question to ask as a 'fixer' type parent, but one that I've had to learn. And ultimately, listening is a privilege.

Respecting their boundaries also means acknowledging their right to make decisions, even if I don't always agree with them. This was one of the most challenging aspects for me. I had to learn to offer guidance and share my perspectives without infringing on their right to make choices. It was about providing them with the tools and insights to make informed decisions rather than making those decisions for them.

Let me be clear: respecting boundaries and privacy doesn't mean disregarding harmful behaviors or decisions. It's about fostering open communication and being a safe space for your teen to come to when ready. And it's about trusting that the values and lessons you've imparted over the years have provided them with a solid moral compass to navigate the complexities of adult life.

Adjusting to this new dynamic was challenging. There were missteps and moments of frustration, but through it all, we kept the lines of communication open. We spoke openly about our expectations and comfort zones. Slowly, we found our balance. Today, as I look at the strong, confident man Ted is growing into, I'm glad I learned to respect his boundaries and privacy. It allowed him to grow, to make mistakes and learn from them, and to become the person he is today. As for Nina, we are still negotiating, and I continue to learn to be as respectful and kind as possible while encouraging mutual respect.

Remember, it's not about letting go entirely but about adjusting your grip, giving them the room to grow, explore, and become their own person while knowing you're there, ready to support them every step of the way. They will appreciate you for it.

Chapter Takeaways

1. Transition from Top-Down Parenting to Mentoring: As your teen matures, shift from being an enforcer of rules to a mentor who guides. This involves walking alongside them, offering advice, and empowering them to make their own decisions.

2. Foster Emotional Intimacy: Investing time in one-on-one conversations and bonding experiences can help build trust and emotional closeness. This foundation of trust enables your teenager to confide in you, knowing they will be understood and supported.

3. Encourage Open Communication: Create a safe space for open dialogue where both parties can share their thoughts, feelings, and concerns without fear of judgment. This contributes to a deeper, more meaningful relationship.

4. Respect Their Independence and Privacy: Acknowledge that your teen is becoming an adult with their own set of experiences, friendships, and challenges. Respecting their personal space and privacy is crucial for fostering trust and independence.

5. Support Personal and Professional Goals: Be a cheerleader for your teen's dreams and ambitions. Offer resources, encouragement, and emotional support, but let them lead their journey.

6. Engage in Shared Activities: Bonding over common interests provides an excellent opportunity for meaningful interactions and conversations. It not only strengthens the relationship but also enriches lives.

7. Be Adaptable and Patient: Transitioning from a top-down parent to a mentor doesn't happen overnight. It requires mutual respect, patience, and open communication.

8. Set and Respect Boundaries: As your child grows into an adult, the dynamics of your relationship will change. Learning to set and respect new boundaries is integral to this evolving relationship.

9. Balance Guidance and Autonomy: While you may have a wealth of experience and advice to offer, it's crucial to strike a balance between guiding your teen and allowing them the autonomy to make their own decisions.

10. Invest in the Relationship: Your relationship with your teen is an ongoing investment that will continue to evolve. Navigating the complexities of this relationship during these transitional years sets the stage for a lifelong bond.

CONCLUSION

Nurturing the Future Today

As I pause to reflect on this exploration we've taken together, I can't help but feel a sense of pride and excitement for you and your teen. We've learned about the developing brain and, with that knowledge, navigated the twists and turns of your teenagers' lives, from academic pressure to fostering independence, from financial literacy to encouraging community involvement, and lastly, instilling resilience and coping skills. This was no small task, but the growth that awaits you and your teenager is vast.

No book can hold all the answers to the enigma that is parenting, particularly during the teenage years. However, through the understanding and application of my seven-step program, you're prepared to face the challenges head-on and lay a solid foundation for a stronger, more fulfilling relationship with your teenager. By fostering open communication, promoting positive habits and essential life skills, and nurturing creativity and personal growth, you can truly influence your teen's life trajectory.

My friend's son Sam was a rebellious teenager, causing his parents sleepless nights. But with the implementation of the principles we've discussed in this book, through our many, many conversations, Sam's parents were able to turn things around. Today, Sam is not just successful in his career, but he also possesses the life skills and emotional intelligence necessary for a fulfilling life. This transformation is the power of effective parenting.

Now, I won't paint an overly rosy picture. Parenting a teenager is hard! You'll have days when you question your decisions and have moments of self-doubt. But remember, no one is asking you to be a perfect parent. Your teen doesn't need perfection. They need your presence, your patience, your understanding, and above all, your unwavering love and support.

The theories and principles explored in this book will serve as your guide, illuminating the path towards a better understanding of your teen and a more enriching relationship.

Be prepared for tough conversations. Take a deep breath, dive in, and give it your all. Be open to learning and unlearning. Embrace the mistakes and cherish the victories. Remember to be patient with your teenager and yourself as you tread this path. Change doesn't happen overnight, but with consistent effort, it will happen. And when the challenging times seem endless, remember those sleepless nights you had with your baby; they passed just as these difficult times will eventually, too.

Remember that your role in your teenager's life is irreplaceable. Even on the toughest days, they look to you for guidance and love. Stand firm in your commitment to nurture their growth and navigate this stage of life together.

I wish you and your teenager growth, happiness, and strengthening of your bond. Your journey to transform the trials of parenting into triumphs begins now.

The challenges of parenting a teenager should not leave you feeling frustrated, helpless, or disconnected. You've got the tools now and have what it takes to build a strong, lasting connection with your teenager. Remember, your greatest strength as a parent is your love for your child. And with that, you can conquer any challenge that comes your way.

Resources

This is not an exhaustive list, but here are some resources, some of which I have mentioned in the text.

Nutrition

Teen Cook: How to Cook What You Want to Eat by Megan and Jill Carle

https://www.amazon.com/Teens-Cook-How-What-Want/dp/1580085849

The Complete Cookbook for Young Chefs by America's Test Kitchen

https://www.amazon.com/Complete-Cookbook-Young-Chefs-Recipes/dp/B09C94JCT9/

Social media

Family Media Agreement example:

https://www.commonsensemedia.org/sites/default/files/featured-content/files/common_sense_family_media_agreement.pdf

www.commonsensemedia.org
www.waittill8th.org

Mental Health

Call 988 Suicide and Crisis Hotline
www.988lifeline.org
www.teentalkapp.org
National Alliance on Mental Health
https://nami.org/Home
https://www.thetrevorproject.org/

Substance Abuse

https://www.samhsa.gov/find-help/national-helpline
www.dea.org/onepill/teens
www.endoverdose.net

Sexual Health

www.plannedparenthood.org

REFERENCES

Here are some key sources and links to data that I found helpful while writing this book.

Chapter 2

The Teen Brain: https://www.nimh.nih.gov/health/publications/the-teen-brain-7-things-to-know

Chapter 3

Nutrition in adolescence: https://pubmed.ncbi.nlm.nih.gov/10036686/#:~:text=Adolescent%20females%20require%20approximately%202200,zinc%2C%20vitamins%2C%20and%20fiber.

Chapter 5

Teen Mental Health Data:

https://www.cdc.gov/childrensmentalhealth/data.html

https://mhanational.org/issues/2023/mental-health-america-youth-data

https://www.unc.edu/posts/2023/01/03/study-shows-habitual-checking-of-social-media-may-impact-young-adolescents-brain-development/#:~:text=The%20study%20findings%20suggest%20that,more%20sensitive%20to%20social%20feedback.

https://www.who.int/news-room/fact-sheets/detail/adolescent-mental-health

https://www.cdc.gov/nchs/products/databriefs/db472.htm#:~:text=Children%20aged%2012%E2%80%9317%20years,%E2%80%9311%20years%20(11.3%25).

https://www.cdc.gov/nchs/data/databriefs/db352-h.pdf

https://www.nimh.nih.gov/health/statistics/any-anxiety-disorder

https://www.nimh.nih.gov/health/statistics/eating-disorders#:~:text=Prevalence%20of%20Eating%20Disorders%20in%20Adolescents,-Based%20on%20diagnostic&text=The%20lifetime%20prevalence%20of%20eating,%25)%20than%20males%20(1.5%25).

Eating Disorders:

https://www.jahonline.org/article/S1054-139X(21)00371-2/pdf

https://publications.aap.org/pediatrics/article/147/1/e2020040279/33504/Identification-and-Management-of-Eating-Disorders?autologincheck=redirected

Family-Based Treatment of Eating Disorders: https://www.ncbi.nlm.nih.gov/pmc/articles/PMC5459462/

Chapter 6

Effects of Nicotine:
https://www.ncbi.nlm.nih.gov/pmc/articles/PMC4363846/
https://www.ncbi.nlm.nih.gov/pmc/articles/PMC1748379/pdf/v009p00313.pdf

E-cigarettes:
https://www.cdc.gov/tobacco/basic_information/e-cigarettes/about-e-cigarettes.html#:~:text=The%20e%2Dcigarette%20aerosol%20that,to%20a%20serious%20lung%20disease

Driving:
https://www.aacap.org/AACAP/Families_and_Youth/Facts_for_Families/FFF-Guide/Helping-Your_Teen-Become-A-Safe-Driver-076.aspx#:~:text=Traffic%20crashes%20are%20the%20%231,motor%20vehicle%20collisions%20each%20year.

Sexual Risk Taking:
Parkes, A., Henderson, M., Wight, D., & Nixon, C. (2011). Is Parenting Associated with Teenagers' Early Sexual Risk-Taking, Autonomy And Relationship with Sexual Partners? *Perspectives on Sexual and Reproductive Health*, *43*(1), 30–40. https://doi.org/10.1363/4303011

Chapter 7

Safe sex:
Whitaker, D. J., Miller, K. S., May, D. C., & Levin, M. L. (1999). Teenage partners' communication about sexual risk and condom use: The importance of Parent-Teenager Discussions. *Family Planning Perspectives*, *31*(3), 117. https://doi.org/10.2307/2991693

Printed in Great Britain
by Amazon